No-Nonsense Credit

An Insider's Guide to
Borrowing Money and
Managing Debt

No-Nonsense Credit

An Insider's Guide to Borrowing Money and Managing Debt

Richard H. Jorgensen

LIBERTY HALL
PRESS™

LIBERTY HALL PRESS books are published by LIBERTY HALL PRESS, an imprint of McGraw-Hill, Inc. Its trademark, consisting of the words ''LIBERTY HALL PRESS'' and the portrayal of Benjamin Franklin, is registered in the United States Patent and Trademark Office.

FIRST EDITION
THIRD PRINTING

Library of Congress Cataloging-in-Publication Data

Jorgensen, Richard H.
No-nonsense credit : an insider's guide to borrowing money and managing debt / by Richard H. Jorgensen.
p.   cm.
Includes index.
ISBN 0-8306-3546-7
1. Consumer credit—Handbooks, manuals, etc.   2. Credit control--Handbooks, manuals, etc.   3. Finance, Personal—Handbooks, manuals. etc. I. Title.
HG3755.J59   1990
332.024'02—dc20   90-13333
                                                                           CIP

For information about other McGraw-Hill materials, call 1-800-2-MCGRAW in the U.S. In other countries call your nearest McGraw-Hill office.

Vice President and Editorial Director: David J. Conti
Book Editor: Shelly Chevalier
Director of Production: Katherine G. Brown
Book Design: Jaclyn J. Boone
Cover Design: Lori E. Schlosser

To my family
Barbara Jorgensen
Mary Jorgensen-Haynes
Susan Jorgensen
Jean Boston
Mark Jorgensen
Nancy Meyer
Paul Jorgensen

Contents

Introduction

CREDIT IS SUCH A HIGHLY SIGNIFICANT PART OF OUR LIVES ON BOTH PERSONAL and business levels. Of this I can speak from experience. Credit has had a powerful impact on my life and has played an important role in my being able to accumulate security and a good standard of living. Let me tell you how credit power has worked for me.

My father died when I was two years old. I was raised by my grandparents in a small, rural midwest village, population 550, during the 1930s and 40s. Mere existence for everyone back then was a struggle. The simple necessities of life were barely affordable to say nothing of any sort of luxury. As a child I remember a five-cent bag of hard candy was something I cherished. For the first 16 years of my life I never saw a dentist or a doctor, not because it wasn't needed, but because neither of these services were available in this small remote village. We couldn't afford a car so there was no way to get to a doctor. Back then when you got sick you lived through it by eating home-made chicken soup, or you died. In my case the chicken soup must have worked.

I certainly knew the humility of being poor. It is difficult to build and develop any sort of self-esteem and self-worth under normal circumstances of growing up, but to overcome the humility of poverty adds tremendously to that burden. So for me it was a difficult task of recognizing any good of myself or my surroundings.

When I left this community at the age of 17 in 1945, I barely had enough money to get out of town. In fact, I hitch-hiked to the big city because I didn't have the bus fare. By then my grandparents were deceased and I was on my own with no adult protecting or aiding me.

Once I got to the big city I entered into a whole new and awesome environment, a world made up of adults, economics, jobs, salaries, and advanced education. I also entered into a world of self-reliance because I was on my own and I knew I had to get going. Once I made the necessary adjustments, especially that of going from a small remote rural village into a big city, I began setting up a plan and way to get out of poverty.

My first and most important discovery of the credit world was to find out I could attend college and pay later—later meaning after I graduated and got a job. Next, I found that education gave me an opportunity to acquire a better-than-average job. I easily moved into the business world, was able ultimately to buy my own business—all done on credit.

Fortunately my business flourished and I was able to buy other small businesses. Since, by using my credit, I have been able to acquire 33 real estate rental properties.

Because I was given the privilege of buying now and paying later, I have reached a lifestyle far beyond that of poverty. Most of this success can be attributed to the trust granted by others that I would fulfill my credit and financial obligations. It has worked for me.

Mine isn't the only Horatio Alger story. This story, of course, could be repeated many times over. Most wealth, other than "old" money wealth, has been acquired basically through this same method—first trust, then credit, financing, mortgages, and repayment.

I'm not telling my story to impress you with my accomplishments. I don't need that. Rather, I am telling you this story to let you see that if I, a common, ordinary, average person just like you meet everyday at your workplace and in your neighborhood, can move about in our free enterprise system and do what I have done, then anyone can do it. It's proof that anyone can rise from the lowest economic level to any level of accomplishment they want.

It is my hope that the information in this book will help you overcome any self-doubt, fears, or weaknesses regarding our credit-financial world. This book, then, is to show you how to care for and use money to your best advantage. This book is about the use of credit power.

1

Credit and
the Good Life

WOULDN'T IT BE NICE IF WE COULD INHERIT ENOUGH MONEY TO LIVE, DO business, invest, and buy whatever we wanted without going in debt? If so, we would all be millionaires. But that isn't the way things are, nor is it the real world of business, finance, and credit. Very few of us inherit this kind of money.

Credit can give us the good things in life

As a matter of fact, most of us have to rely totally on credit for almost everything we do. Our existence depends on our being able to buy now and pay later, whether it's for our light and gas bill, a new car, a home, investing in a business, or buying real estate. It's a known fact that over 50 percent of everything purchased today is bought on credit. Can you imagine trying to buy a home or a car, or just pay for the services of everyday living and not have the ability to charge?

Not only can we charge our everyday living expenses, but with credit we can have access to some of the good things in life—vacation homes, trips, and luxuries. But more important, credit provides us with the ability to have complete control over our financial destiny. In other words, we can build our own future and fortune to whatever magnitude we desire.

Changing times
have created a new class

It hasn't always been that way, that we could just go out and buy whatever we wanted and charge it. There was a time when credit was considered a luxury, something only for the rich. Of course, back in those days there were only two classes, the rich and the poor. And for the poor, credit was non-existent. In fact, credit was considered unethical and debt was strictly taboo. Most of us have heard about debtors prisons—if the bill wasn't paid the debtor was put behind bars—which was part of the credit taboo system that existed.

We have come a long way since then. In the 1940s, credit created a whole new generation in our free enterprise system. We know and are a part of that generation called the American middle class. With credit each and everyone was able to buy cars, refrigerators, a home, and even some luxuries.

With the use of credit, that generation was indeed able to move into middle-class America. Some rose above the middle-class level and became a part of the wealthy class simply by shrewdly using credit and borrowing power.

This credit power, and the over-all credit economy, certainly represents our free enterprise system at its best. We have the freedom to do those things that better our lives, and credit provides us with a way to accumulate wealth for the sake of personal security. The free-enterprise system, along with the credit economy gives us the ability to grow however we wish, with no barriers and no restrictions.

Credit is a privilege and not a right

Credit is not a right but is a privilege. Credit is not something you can demand without question. Neither can credit be forced on us, and we have the right to refuse credit at any time. Anyone can go through life existing fairly comfortably without borrowing and paying mortgage payments. However, most of us need credit to maintain our lifestyle and realize that it would be very difficult to accumulate wealth without the use of credit.

My theory about building wealth through investments is to use credit to the maximum and buy whatever we can afford. My theory also is that there is no better time than right now to do it. There has never been a more opportune time for anyone to grab the golden ring of success. It's there to be had and there is absolutely no limit.

Your future and your
fortune are in your hands

Your future and your fortune, whatever they might be and whatever your desires are, are in your hands. You have complete control over your own destiny. It is a matter of learning how to use the tools available to reach that goal.

As I look back at the investments I have made—home, business, real estate, and a good standard of living—as I have pursued each and every accomplishment, never once have there been any restrictions. There were no governmental agencies looking over me, no bureaucratic red tape to untangle, and no competitors driving me up a wall. As a matter of fact, throughout my business career my competitors for the most part have been my driving force. Without them I would and could have become slovenly. The only restrictions I ever had were those that I placed on myself.

Those restrictions consisted of self-doubt, the fear of failure, and the inability to make quick decisions. I have a feeling that if there hadn't been that self-doubt and that inability to make decisions there could have been 333 rental properties or even 3333. But that's history.

2

How to Make Your Credit Work for You

NOW THAT WE KNOW HOW ESSENTIAL CREDIT IS FOR US TO FUNCTION AND survive in our financial world, it is equally important to know and realize how important *good* credit is, not only to survive, but to be able to acquire the good things in life.

Building a good credit record

As we have already pointed out, credit can be used to buy goods and services, a car, household goods, a home, investments, a business, and just about anything we want and can afford. In fact, it's possible to go out to dinner this evening and pay later, simply by using your credit card.

It has also been mentioned that credit gives us the ability to establish security, build a future, accumulate wealth, and to grab the golden ring of success—however, all that depends on having *good* credit.

This being the case, let's see how your personal credit history can work for you in your everyday life and in the marketplace.

Your credit history and how it works

Your credit history—how each of you have lived up to your agreement of paying obligations and commitments, how you pay your bills—is information that is gathered and stored by credit reporting agencies all over the country. Anyone who has used credit at any time or any place in all likelihood has a complete file stored in a computerized reporting agency. In fact, that file is probably on file right in your home community.

We live in a computer age which means that our credit history is stored and readily available to any credit grantor whenever and wherever we apply. You can live in the midwest, travel to New York City, and apply for credit at Macy's or Gimbel's and be approved right there on the spot. The credit manager at Macy's or Gimbel's, with one mere touch of a computer key, can have your file brought into their credit office within seconds.

The importance of good credit

Having that credit file readily available certainly isn't all that bad. In fact, if it's instantly available, and the record is good, we can buy what we want when we want it.

That record, for all practical purposes, is the primary source of information that each and every credit manager uses in determining our creditworthiness. This file is used for approval or denial. Therefore, your credit record, and your credit history, should be cared for with great concern, just as you would care for any other valuable asset or investment. When I say it should be cared for I mean this: If we make a credit commitment it's important to live up to that commitment. In other words, the obligation you make must be paid back as agreed.

Your entire creditworthiness and credibility depends on how you pay your bills. That is what constitutes your credit history and your credit file. That's how the credit system works. It's that simple.

The credit report and its meaning

Now let's see exactly what information is stored in a credit file and what an actual credit report looks like.

The following sample reports are routine and standard reports that come from almost any credit reporting agency. They are fairly simple to understand but there is an explanation of what the various symbols mean. The symbols are there simply for brevity, not secrecy. The name and dates of the reports, which by the way are actual files, have been changed but the ratings and information is factual. On the back of each report is a set of directions explaining the report (Figs. 2-1 and 2-2).

What you've seen is an actual report pulled out of a credit reporting agency computer and then written on a standard reporting form.

The information in this particular report discloses that the individual has all good ratings, which means all credit obligations have been taken care of as agreed. This is the kind of report that makes immediate credit available and opens the doors of the credit world. It's the kind of report that can and will produce some solid financial results. It's the kind of a report bankers like to see.

NAME AND ADDRESS OF CREDIT BUREAU MAKING REPORT

☐ SINGLE REFERENCE ☐ IN FILE REPORT ☐ TRADE REPORT

CREDIT BUREAU OF ANYTOWN
1131 MAIN STREET
ANYTOWN, ANYSTATE 12345

☐ FULL REPORT ☐ EMPLOY & TRADE REPORT ☐ PREVIOUS RESIDENCE REPORT

☒ OTHER REAL ESTATE LOAN

FOR ┌ FIRST NATIONAL BANK 1234 MAIN STREET ANYTOWN, ANYSTATE 56789 ┘	**Date Received** 0-0-00 **Date Mailed** 0-0-00 **In File Since** 0000 **Inquired As:**	**CONFIDENTIAL** crediscope® REPORT ⬛ Member Associated Credit Bureaus, Inc.

REPORT ON:	LAST NAME CONSUMER	FIRST NAME ROBERT J.	INITIAL	SOCIAL SECURITY NUMBER 123-45-6789	SPOUSE'S NAME BETTY R.
ADDRESS:	CITY 1234 ANY STREET	STATE: ANYTOWN, ANYSTATE	ZIP CODE 56789	SINCE: 0000	SPOUSE'S SOCIAL SECURITY NO. 987-65-4321

COMPLETE TO HERE FOR TRADE REPORT AND SKIP TO CREDIT HISTORY

PRESENT EMPLOYER: XYZ CORPORATION	POSITION HELD: MANAGER-OWNER	SINCE: 25 yrs	DATE EMPLOY VERIFIED 0000	EST. MONTHLY INCOME $ 4000

COMPLETE TO HERE FOR EMPLOYMENT AND TRADE REPORT AND SKIP TO CREDIT HISTORY

DATE OF BIRTH 10-10-40	NUMBER OF DEPENDENTS INCLUDING SELF: FOUR	☒ OWNS OR BUYING HOME	☐ RENTS HOME	OTHER: (EXPLAIN) ☐

FORMER ADDRESS:	CITY:	STATE:	FROM:	TO:

FORMER EMPLOYER:	POSITION HELD:	FROM:	TO:	EST. MONTHLY INCOME $

SPOUSE'S EMPLOYER: ACME COMPANY	POSITION HELD: SECRETARY	SINCE: 20 years	DATE EMPLOY VERIFIED 0-0-00	EST. MONTHLY INCOME $ 1000

CREDIT HISTORY *(Complete this section for all reports)*

WHOSE	KIND OF BUSINESS AND ID CODE	DATE REPORTED AND METHOD OF REPORTING	DATE OPENED	DATE OF LAST PAYMENT	HIGHEST CREDIT OR LAST CONTRACT	BALANCE OWING	PAST DUE AMOUNT	NO. OF PAYMENTS	NO. MONTHS HISTORY REVIEWED	30-59 DAYS ONLY	60-89 DAYS ONLY	90 DAYS AND OVER	TYPE & TERMS (MANNER OF PAYMENT)	REMARKS
J	Bank Manual	0-00	0000	$34000	$6470	0	36	36	0	0	0	Installment	$430 mo
J	Bank Manual	0-00	0000	$20000	$7110	0	24	24	0	0	0	Installment	$260 mo
	Bank Manual	0-00	0000	$5191	0	0	36	36	0	0	0	Installment	$150 mo
J	Sears Auto	0-00	0000	$1429	0	0	12	12	0	0	0	Revolving	$ 35 mo
J	Mst CrAuto	0-00	0000	$2899	0	0	12	12	0	0	0	Revolving	$ 25 mo
	Bank Manual	0-00	0000	Applicant maintains medium five figure business checking account and high four figure personal checking account with a five figure savings account.										

PUBLIC RECORDS: Court records have been checked, nothing recorded.

Fig. 2-1. This is a standard credit report used universally by most credit reporting bureaus. The name and address and other identifiable features of the report have been changed but the financial and credit report information is factual. This is an example of an excellent credit report.

TERMS OF SALE

Open Account (30 days or 90 days) . . . . O
Revolving or Option (Open-end a/c) . . . . R
Installment (fixed number of payments) I

COMMON LANGUAGE FOR CONSUMER CREDIT

CURRENT MANNER OF PAYMENT (Using Payments Past Due or Age from Due Date)	Type of Account		
	O	R	I
Too new to rate; approved but not used	0	0	0
Pays (or paid) within 30 days of payment due date, or not over one payment past due	1	1	1
Pays (or paid) in more than 30 days from the payment due date, but not more than 60 days, or not more than two payments past due	2	2	2
Pays (or paid) in more than 60 days from payment due date, but not more than 90 days, or three payments past due	3	3	3
Pays (or paid) in more than 90 days from payment due date, but not more than 120 days, or four payments past due	4	4	4
Pays (or paid) in more than 120 days or more than four payments past due	5	5	5
Making regular payments under debtor's plan or similar arrangement	7	7	7
Repossession. (Indicate if it is a voluntary return of merchandise by the consumer)	8	8	8
Bad debt	9	9	9

—Revised 1988

KIND OF BUSINESS CLASSIFICATION

Code	Kind of Business	Code	Kind of Business
A	Automotive	N	National Credit Card Companies and Air Lines
B	Banks	O	Oil Companies
C	Clothing	P	Personal Services Other Than Medical
D	Department and Variety	Q	Mail Order Houses
F	Finance	R	Real Estate and Public Accommodations
G	Groceries	S	Sporting Goods
H	Home Furnishings	T	Farm and Garden Supplies
I	Insurance	U	Utilities and Fuel
J	Jewelry and Cameras	V	Government
K	Contractors	W	Wholesale
L	Lumber, Building Material, Hardware	X	Advertising
M	Medical and Related Health	Y	Collection Services
		Z	Miscellaneous

A. Column 1, "Whose Account", provides a means of showing how a credit grantor maintains the account for ECOA purposes. Examples: 0—Undesignated, 1—Individual account for individual use, 2—Joint account contractual liability, 3—Authorized user spouse, 4—Joint, 5—Co-maker, 6—"On behalf of" account, 7—Maker, 8—Indiv. Acct. of spouse, 9—Subject is no longer associated with account.

B. Column 3, "Method of Reporting", indicates how a trade item was placed in file: A—computer tape or TVS, M—Manual.

C. When inserting dates, use month and year only (Example: 12-88)

D. Manner of Payment using Common Language coding (I-$175-1) will be printed in column 14 for in-file trade items which do not contain information for credit history.

E. Remarks codes (Examples)

ACC—Account closed by consumer.
AJP —Adjustment pending.
BKL —Account included in Bankruptcy.
CCA—Consumer counseling account. Consumer has retained the services of an organization which is directing payment of his accounts.
CLA —Placed for collection.
DIS —Dispute following resolution.
DRP —Dispute. Resolution pending.
JUD —Judgment obtained for balance shown.
MOV—Moved. Left no forwarding address.
PPL —Paid P & L Account.

PRL —Profit and loss write-off.
RLD —Repossession. Paid by dealer.
RLP —Repossession. Proceeds applied to debt.
RPO —Repossession.
RRE —Repossession, redeemed.
RVD —Returned voluntarily. Paid by dealer.
RVN —Returned voluntarily.
RVP —Returned voluntarily, proceeds applied to debt.
RVR —Returned voluntarily, redeemed.
STL —Plate stolen or lost.
WEP —Account Included in Chapter 13 Plan for Adjustment of Debts.

F. Account Numbers, if shown, should appear on second line just below each trade item.

G. Disputes and comments associated with specific trade lines should be printed on second or third line in cases where account numbers are printed.

Fig. 2-2. This information is found on the back of all credit reports and reveals the various codes that are used in making up the report.

All is not flawless and perfect in credit reports

There's more because all reports aren't good. A copy of a report, again with actual information, of an individual having some financial problems illustrates this point (Fig. 2-3).

This report was requested by a bank for a home mortgage. You will note at the bottom of the report that a previous home was lost through a mortgage foreclosure. From this we can assume that the new report is for the purchase of a different home.

As you read this report you will discover the individual has a reported total indebtedness of $25,966. That doesn't take into consideration that there are probably other debts that have not been reported to the reporting agency. This indebtedness of $25,966 consisting of credit cards, appliance loans, department store bills, car, and other loans is only part of the story. There are the routine everyday bills of doctors, dentists, utilities, etc that are not included. Nor does it consider a home mortgage. Payments on the bills exceed $900 a month. As you can see there is an income of $2500 a month which reveals some serious financial problems ahead.

The report also reveals that some of the bills and payments have been running 60 and 90 days past due. About the time these payments started running past due there were applications for more credit cards. It appears as though the current cards were filled to the maximum and more cards were needed to cover outstanding debts and expenses. This is certainly a prime example of how some of us can get into financial and credit trouble. It's simply a case of over-spending.

Put yourself in the position of the credit manager or loan officer who has to make a decision on the basis of the information in this report. Would you grant a loan with this kind of history?

And there's still more. What we have seen so far is a good credit report and a marginal report. The following report illustrates very vividly how credit can really get out of hand. It's a case of spending and not having sufficient income to meet the obligations. And most of all, this is a history of an individual who obviously has not taken credit very seriously.

This report reveals a consistent record of tardiness in paying all obligations. There are a number of accounts for collection, of which some are paid, others not paid. There is also an unsatisfied judgment in the amount of $550. Here is a story and history of serious financial problems. It appears that the only solution for someone in this kind of shape is to become serious about their financial situation and quit spending.

This report was ordered by the Federal Housing Administration (FHA) for a government-guaranteed home loan. If you were the loan officer would you approve the loan?

These reports and the information in them is typical of most reports stored in the various reporting agencies. Your file is basically the same and is also stored in one of these agencies. Incidentally, only a credit reporting agency stores credit

NAME AND ADDRESS OF CREDIT BUREAU MAKING REPORT

☐ SINGLE REFERENCE ☐ IN FILE REPORT ☐ TRADE REPORT

☐ FULL REPORT ☐ EMPLOY & TRADE REPORT ☐ PREVIOUS RESIDENCE REPORT

☒ OTHER __REAL ESTATE MORTGAGE__

CREDIT BUREAU
1131 MAIN STREET
ANYTOWN, ANYSTATE 12345

FOR

FIRST NATIONAL BANK
1133 MAIN STREET
ANYTOWN, ANYSTATE 12345

Date Received
0-0-00

Date Mailed
0-5-00

In File Since
0000

Inquired As:
JOINT

CONFIDENTIAL
crediscope® REPORT

Member
Associated Credit Bureaus, Inc.

REPORT ON: LAST NAME	FIRST NAME INITIAL	SOCIAL SECURITY NUMBER	SPOUSE'S NAME
CONSUMER ROBERT G.		123-45-6789	BETTY R.

ADDRESS: CITY	STATE:	ZIP CODE	SINCE:	SPOUSE'S SOCIAL SECURITY NO.
1234 ANYSTREET ANYTOWN, ANYSTATE 12345				987-65-4321

COMPLETE TO HERE FOR TRADE REPORT AND SKIP TO CREDIT HISTORY

PRESENT EMPLOYER:	POSITION HELD:	SINCE:	DATE EMPLOY VERIFIED	EST. MONTHLY INCOME
XYZ CORPORATION	ASST DEPT MGR	00-00	0000	$ 2500

COMPLETE TO HERE FOR EMPLOYMENT AND TRADE REPORT AND SKIP TO CREDIT HISTORY

DATE OF BIRTH	NUMBER OF DEPENDENTS INCLUDING SELF:			
5-25-50	4	☐ OWNS OR BUYING HOME	☐ RENTS HOME	OTHER: (EXPLAIN) ☒ Purchasing

FORMER ADDRESS:	CITY:	STATE:	FROM:	TO:
4321 ANYSTREET	ANYTOWN ANYSTATE		0000	0000

FORMER EMPLOYER:	POSITION HELD:	FROM:	TO:	EST. MONTHLY INCOME
ABC & ASSOCIATES	SALES PERSON	0000	0000	$ 1285

SPOUSE'S EMPLOYER:	POSITION HELD:	SINCE:	DATE EMPLOY VERIFIED	EST. MONTHLY INCOME
BIG CITY DEPARTMENT STORE	CASHIER	0000	0000	$ 1200

CREDIT HISTORY (*Complete this section for all reports*)

WHOSE	KIND OF BUSINESS AND ID CODE	DATE REPORTED AND METHOD OF REPORTING	DATE OPENED	DATE OF LAST PAYMENT	HIGHEST CREDIT OR LAST CONTRACT	BALANCE OWING	PAST DUE AMOUNT	NO. OF PAYMENTS	NO. MONTHS HISTORY REVIEWED	30-59 DAYS ONLY	60-89 DAYS ONLY	90 DAYS AND OVER	TYPE & TERMS (MANNER OF PAYMENT)	REMARKS
	Bank	Manual	0-00	0-00	$2900	$2550	0	24	16	2	1	0	$57 mo	Installment
	Bank	Autom	0-00	0-00	$2300	$1600	0	24	12	1	0	0	$51 mo	Installment
	GE Cr	Manual	0-00	0-00	$517	$400	0	18	9	0	0	0	$27 mo	Installment
	Applia	Manual	0-00	0-00	$900	$536	0	36	18	1	1	0	$36 mo	Installment
	J C Pen	Auto	0-00	0-00	$210	$102	0	24	12	1	0	0	$19 mo	Revolving
	Sears	Auto	0-00	0-00	$820	$465	0	36	18	2	1	0	$34 mo	Installment
	Wards	Auto	0-00	0-00	$194	0	0	12	12	0	0	0	$12 mo	Revolving
	Cr Union	Manual	0-00	0-00	$9000	$7345	0	36	8	0	0	0	$285 mo	Installment
	RE Loan	Manual	0-00	0-00	$23,000	0	0	30y	18	0	0	0	$245 mo	Installment
	Car Loan	Manu	0-00	0-00	$15700	$13000	0	36	10	0	0	0	$517 mo	Installment

COURT RECORDS: Foreclosure proceedings started 0-000 Knudsen Real Estate Mortgage Company
Property sold, mortgage foreclosure satisfied 0-0000
BANK   Manual 0-00 0-00   Maintains medium three figure checking account satisfactorily
        Savings account balance zero with fluctuating balance
INQUIRIES: Master card 0-00, Visa 0-00, Discover 0-00, Ford Motor Credit Corp 0-00.
        General Electric Credit Corporation 0-00, Whirlpool Credit Corporation 0-00

Fig. 2-3. This is a report for a home loan. As you can see by reading the information on the report this individual has had some credit problems which includes a foreclosure. The credit manager dealing with this report will have some problems making a decision on a long term mortgage.

NAME AND ADDRESS OF CREDIT BUREAU MAKING REPORT

☐ SINGLE REFERENCE	☐ IN FILE REPORT	☐ TRADE REPORT
☐ FULL REPORT	☐ EMPLOY & TRADE REPORT	☐ PREVIOUS RESIDENCE REPORT
☒ OTHER __REAL ESTATE MORTGAGE__		

CREDIT BUREAU
1131 MAIN STREET
ANYTOWN, ANYSTATE 12345

FOR

FEDERAL HOUSING ADMINISTRATION
1132 MAIN STREET
ANYTOWN, ANYSTATE 12345

Date Received	CONFIDENTIAL
0-0-00	crediscope® REPORT
Date Mailed	
0-5-00	
In File Since	Member
0000	Associated Credit Bureaus, Inc
Inquired As:	
JOINT	

| REPORT ON: LAST NAME | FIRST NAME | INITIAL | SOCIAL SECURITY NUMBER | SPOUSE'S NAME |
| CONSUMER | ROBERT | G. | 123-45-6789 | BETTY R. |

| ADDRESS: CITY | STATE: | ZIP CODE | SINCE: | SPOUSE'S SOCIAL SECURITY NO. |
| 1234 ANYSTREET | ANYTOWN, ANYSTATE 12345 | | 0000 | 987-65-4321 |

COMPLETE TO HERE FOR TRADE REPORT AND SKIP TO CREDIT HISTORY

| PRESENT EMPLOYER: | POSITION HELD: | SINCE: | DATE EMPLOY VERIFIED | EST. MONTHLY INCOME |
| ABC FOODS | NIGHT SUPERVISOR | 4-1-00 | 8-2-00 | $ 2,000 |

COMPLETE TO HERE FOR EMPLOYMENT AND TRADE REPORT AND SKIP TO CREDIT HISTORY

| DATE OF BIRTH | NUMBER OF DEPENDENTS INCLUDING SELF: 3 | | | OTHER: (EXPLAIN) |
| 5-25-60 | | ☐ OWNS OR BUYING HOME | ☐ RENTS HOME | ☒ BUYING |

| FORMER ADDRESS: | CITY: | STATE: | FROM: | TO: |
| 56789 ANYSTREET | ANYTOWN II, ANYSTATE | | 0000 | 0000 |

| FORMER EMPLOYER: | POSITION HELD: | FROM: | TO: | EST. MONTHLY INCOME |
| ABC COMPUTER | PLANT EMPLOYEE | 0000 | 0000 | $ 1200 |

| SPOUSE'S EMPLOYER: | POSITION HELD: | SINCE: | DATE EMPLOY VERIFIED | EST. MONTHLY INCOME |
| ABC DISCOUNT STORE | SALES CLERK | 0000 | 0000 | $ 600 |

CREDIT HISTORY (Complete this section for all reports)

WHOSE	KIND OF BUSINESS AND ID CODE	DATE REPORTED AND METHOD OF REPORTING	DATE OPENED	DATE OF LAST PAYMENT	HIGHEST CREDIT OR LAST CONTRACT	PRESENT STATUS BALANCE OWING	PAST DUE AMOUNT	NO. OF PAYMENTS	HISTORICAL STATUS NO. MONTHS HISTORY REVIEWED	TIMES PAST DUE 30-59 DAYS ONLY	60-89 DAYS ONLY	90 DAYS AND OVER	TYPE & TERMS (MANNER OF PAYMENT)	REMARKS
	Dept St	Manual	0-00	0000	$178	$105	$25	15	10	6	2	2	$25 mo	Revolving
	Dept St	Manual	0-00	0000	$295	$220	0	18	12	2	1	3	$28 mo	Revolving
	J C Pen	Auto	0-00	0000	$230	$140	0	16	11	1	1	0	$22 mo	Revolving
	Student Loan	Auto	0-00	0000	$1200	$800	$36	36	16	2	2	1	$18 mo	Installment
	Car Ln	Manual	0-00	0000	$8200	$7000	0	36	14	1	1	0	$86 mo	Installment
	Grocery	Manual	0-00	0000	$86	Check written insufficient funds turned over for collection and paid								
	Hospital	Manual	0-00	0000	$376	Account not paid to hospital, turned over for collection and paid								
	Dentist	Manual	0-00	0000	$116	Account not paid to dentist, turned over for collection and paid								
	Clothing	Manual	0-00	0000	$30	Account not paid to clothing store, turned over for collection, not paid								
	Garage	Manual	0-00	0000	$160	Account not paid to garage, turned over for collection, not paid								
	Bank	Manual	0-00	0000		Maintains a low three figure checking account, 7 checks returned insufficient funds returned in past year								

COURT RECORD: Judgment dated 0-00 to XYZ Apartments $550 for rent, judgment not satisfied
Judgment dated 0-00 to LPZ Doctor $220 for service, judgment not satisfied

This information is furnished in response to an inquiry for the purpose of evaluating credit risks. It has been obtained from sources deemed reliable, the accuracy of which this organization does not guarantee. The inquirer has agreed to indemnify the reporting bureau for any damage arising from misuse of this information, and this report is furnished in reliance upon that indemnity. It must be held in strict confidence, and must not be revealed to the subject reported on, except as required by law.

FORM 2000-5/80

Fig. 2-4. This is an example of a report with negative credit history, including accounts for collections and judgments. A credit manager will have little difficulty in making a decision after reading this kind of report.

information so there's no reason to look any other place. Your record isn't hidden under a rock someplace.

Credit reporting agencies keep files on everyone who uses credit. However, they are not required to establish a credit file on anyone. This is entirely up to each individual. This, however, is not difficult or complicated. If you have no file go to the nearest reporting agency (check the yellow pages) and ask that agency to set up your file. This may cost a few dollars but if you expect to use credit it is a good investment. (A later chapter on credit reporting agencies reveals more information about how they work.)

Don't take your credit record for granted

Once your file is established the next step is taking good care of it. As you can see by the illustrated reports, credit can have a powerful and major influence on your financial life and can in fact control your entire future investment plans. It's a serious business.

There are some who aren't concerned about their credit report and don't take it too seriously. There are others who don't pay too much attention to what's going on with their file and their ratings until it's too late. By the time it is too late they have no idea how much this can affect their well being. Then if it's not good they don't know what to do. That total complacency either slows down or stops the process and can sometimes keep us from doing the things we want to do and buying the things we want to buy.

Then there are others who think their credit record should be held as a secret document—that it's no one's business. They feel anyone "snooping" around in their file is guilty of invasion of privacy.

Your credit record should be a proud possession

Those thoughts and ideas about one's credit record are all well and good, but this does not represent the way one should look at this highly valuable asset. In the first place, you should make sure your file and record is in good order and that the payment record is concise, clear, and filled with good, (only you can control the good part) prompt ratings. Secondly, you should, if the record is good, consider that file a proud possession. You don't have to advertise it in the newspaper or shout it from the housetops, but it doesn't do any good to hold it in total secrecy.

By freeing up your credit report, there are many things that can be done. Let's see how you can put it to use.

How to use good credit

I'm not going to tell you about the borrowing power of the giant corporations or how venture capital works because I don't know. But what I do know is how credit can and does work for everyday people just like you and me. I know how credit works for those people who have to borrow money, have to make payments, and have to stretch every dollar in order to succeed in whatever venture they undertake. I know this because I've dealt with the real life stories of individuals who have put their credit to good use. A few of them follow. The first is about good friends of mine, Mark and Jean, who experienced an exciting success story.

A great deal of Mark and Jean's success can be attributed to the fact that they maintained a good credit record. I do want to add however, that their credit and buying power wasn't the only ingredient of their success story. Mark has many personal attributes that were certainly significant in the total success story, including a natural talent and ability to make precise, quick, and good decisions. That's an important characteristic for any person in business to have. In addition, he is what one can classify as a mover and shaker. He really gets things done.

The movers and shakers do get things done

Movers and shakers are the kind of people who go out and find opportunities. They don't just sit around waiting for them to happen. There's no doubt that there is an opportunity out there for each and everyone of us but most of us don't take the time to go out and find it. Movers and shakers will tell you that if you miss the boat and don't find—and take—that opportunity when it comes along it's because you don't care, don't have the courage, or haven't taken care of your financial affairs.

Mark, being a mover and shaker, really has made things happen. He and Jean started their business career in the 1950's—that being a small dry-cleaning plant. During the 50s and 60s they made a good living, raised a family, but, as with most of us, it was a month-to-month proposition. Often it was a struggle to meet the business as well as personal obligations and bills. Each month after the bills were paid there wasn't much left over for any venture capital.

One asset that Mark and Jean both diligently made an effort to protect was their credit record. They paid their obligations as agreed and this counted heavily in their future plans as you will see.

The thought occurred to Mark that there must be some business that would and could work in conjunction with the dry-cleaning business. As he searched for ideas he came up with a jewel. What about a formal-wear rental business? After all, he already had a store in a good business location and with a few adjustments could start this new business. In addition to that, the major expenses in a formal wear business are cleaning, pressing, alterations, and repairing. He had it all, right there.

He and his family laid out the plans. The first step was to remodel the dry cleaning store and set up a show room for the formal wear. The remodeling money was readily available because the banker approved the loan practically without question.

The next step was getting the formal wear inventory. Here Mark was totally dependent on his credit. But it was no problem and the formal wear companies approved a $100,000 starting inventory strictly on Mark's credit record. He was off and running.

The business was an instant success. In fact, right from the start there was sufficient income to pay off the inventory long before due. This meant there was some real potential out there for this kind of business. The next thought was expansion.

And expansion it was. Relying on his credit, Mark went to a neighboring city and opened a second store. This too was an immediate success and from that point on it's been a success story of constant growth. Today they have eight branch formal-wear stores and are doing very well.

Make your credit work for you

Paul and Sue came to me and asked for advice on how to start an investment program that would enhance their net worth and their future financial growth. They were looking for something that would not take a lot of money or a lot of time, and something they could count on for financial growth.

My first suggestion to them was to find out what kind of a credit record they had. I indicated to them that this could determine what kind of an investment program they could get into—with good credit the sky is the limit.

They did indeed have a good credit record. Once this was established, the next step was finding a bank or loaning institution that would back them. I suggested to them that they might be better off if they put all their eggs in one basket and use just one bank. Put all their accounts, checking, saving, loans, house mortgage and investment program with the one bank. This could easily enhance their chances of getting future financing.

The next move was to start looking for the right kind of an investment. There are of course a number of ways to go. There can be a stock and bond investment program which is something that doesn't take management and can be a good income earner. Also, as a young couple they could consider a small business expansion. And another alternative would be to start a regular savings account. But my personal preference for investing is real estate. I just feel it's got the best potential for financial growth because of appreciation, equity, and tax write-off capability.

I recommended to them that they start looking for some kind of property they could handle. I did stress to them that with real estate it takes time, that it's not a get-rich-quick business. But I told them that those rent checks keep coming in every month and eventually pay off the mortgage, which builds equity, which constitutes net worth. Equity is about as good a savings account as one can find.

After I analyzed the situation with Mark and Sue I was sure they could easily handle real estate. It was something within their borrowing power, real estate doesn't take time away from work, and it could be a natural for them. As a starter I suggested they first learn everything they could about real estate investing. There are some good books out there, comparatively inexpensive, that cover the fundamentals of real estate investing.

REAL ESTATE NOTEBOOK

By ROBERT J. BRUSS

10 best real estate books

Wen I talk with home buyers and real estate investors, I am often asked to recommend the best real estate books. Since I read at least one realty book every two weeks, I see the best and worst books on my favorite topic. Today I would like to share the best books.

With advance apologies to authors who wrote excellent books which didn't make the list, here are the 10 best real estate books, in no particular order. All are available in stock or by special order at local bookstores unless otherwise noted:

(1) "HOW I TURNED $1,000 INTO $5 MILLION IN REAL ESTATE," by William Nickerson (Simon and Schuster). This is the classic granddaddy of real estate books. Although slightly outdated, the basic principles are as solid as ever. Nickerson advocates buying sound, well-located property in need of fix-up. After upgrading, he recommends pyramiding equity by making tax-deferred exchanges for bigger properties. The sequel to this book is "NICKERSON'S NO-RISK FORMULA FOR REAL ESTATE WEALTH" (Simon and Schuster), also an excellent book.

(2) "NOTHING DOWN," by Robert G. Allen (Simon and Schuster). This book revolutionized real estate finance. Based on the principles taught by Jack Miller and John Schaub in their seminar, "Making It Big on Little Deals," Allen wrote his book and developed his own seminar on how to buy a home and investment property with little or no cash from the buyer's pocket. Allen's book outlines dozens of ways to acquire real estate if you are short of cash and how to find bargain property for sale by motivated sellers.

(3) "HOW TO GET RICH IN REAL ESTATE," by Robert W. Kent (Prentice-Hall). First published in 1961, this classic book is still available in paperback. It explains the basic principles of buying small rental properties, which Kent calls "Aunt Tobies." He explains in simple terms the basic theory of how real estate investors can earn big profits.

(4) "HIDDEN WEALTH IN LOCAL REAL ESTATE," by Richard H. Jorgensen (Amacom-American Management Association). The author invests in the tiny town of Marshall, Minn., where he has developed real estate investment principles which are applicable nationwide. The book is liberally spiced with photos to show examples of Jorgensen's ideas. If Jorgensen can succeed in his small town, anyone can.

(5) "THE REALTY BLUE BOOK," by Robert De Heer (Professional Publishing Company, 122 Paul Dr., San Rafael, Calif. 94903, $22). This annual real estate book is very special. It began 22 years ago as a compilation of real estate loan amortization tables. De Heer, a real estate salesman, then added some real estate forms and phrases which he found valuable in his sales work. Over the years the book has evolved into the most authoritative source of real estate contract sales information. It includes basic contract forms, explanations of the latest real estate tax laws, finance details, checklists, clauses, exchange agreements, options, leases, financial tables, and more.

(6) "HOUSEWISE," by Suzanne Brangham (Crown Publishers), now available in paperback. Brangham wrote a classic book about how to make big profits by acquiring run-down property begging for renovation. Starting with the toughest of all properties, condominiums, she shows how to renovate with a profit motive. Never losing sight of the bottom line, Brangham guides readers through the maze of how to create improved housing while making large profits. Women especially love this book but men are allowed to read it, too.

(7) "AGGRESSIVE TAX AVOIDANCE FOR REAL ESTATE INVESTORS," by John T. Reed (Reed Publishing). Each year Jack Reed updates his classic tax guide for real estate investors. He explains the basics of how the tax laws benefit property owners, how the IRS and the court system work, and the tax breaks available to realty investors. Reed follows tax laws; he is not one of those weirdo tax protestors. But he emphasizes the gray areas of realty taxation and how property owners can maximize their tax benefits, such as by making tax-deferred exchanges instead of selling and being subject to taxation.

(8) "LANDLORDING," by Leigh Robinson (Express Publishing). This is by far the best book available explaining the practical day-to-day details of how to manage investment properties. Robinson shares his experiences in a humorous style. The book is liberally spiced with cartoons to make the reading easy and fun. Property management is the dull side of earning real estate profits but Robinson shares his profitable advice while making the reading as lively as possible.

(9) "INVEST IN DEBT," by Jim Napier (Jim Napier Inc., P.O. Box F, Chipley, Fla. 32428, $12). Real estate investors who dislike negotiating property purchases, managing properties, and worrying whether tenants will pay the rent love this book. It offers an alternative and often far more profitable realty investment. Napier relates, in very basic style, the secret world of discounted mortgage profits. He explains how to buy existing mortgages from individuals at yields of 15 to 25 percent, sometimes higher. Although Napier is super-smart, he wrote this book in plain language which any reader can understand. By far, this is the best book on discounted mortgage investing.

(10) "TRUMP: THE ART OF THE DEAL," by Donald J. Trump (Random House). This brilliant book which smoothly reads like a novel shows how to think like a real estate tycoon. While Trump is not known for his modesty, he is famous for putting together impossible real estate transactions.

Fig. 2-5. Credit can make wealth and can be used for buying investment real estate. Here is a list of the ten best real estate books for small investors by real estate author-investor-columnist Robert Bruss.

The books I recommend come from Robert Bruss, syndicated columnist with the Tribune Media Service. He writes a weekly column for 300 newspapers all over the country. In addition Bruss is a real estate author and has written *The Smart Investor's Guide to Real Estate*. I think he knows the real estate business about as well as anyone I know. He's not one of those get-rich-quick artists but more of a down-to-earth, practical, commonsense advocate.

In a recent column Bruss listed the 10 best real estate books. I consider it an honor and am proud to have been included on this list of books. These are the ones I recommend to anyone who's interested in real estate investing.

Good advice for landlords

Reno Gazette-Journal   Saturday, January 21, 1989—8

The No-Nonsense Landlord, by Richard H. Jorgensen, Published by Liberty House, a division of Tab Books Inc., Blue Ridge Summit, Pa., 1988, $22.95, 178 pages, available in stock or by special order at local bookstores.

By Robert Bruss

If you are a novice landlord looking for guidance on how to get started on the road to riches or you have started but are losing momentum, read Richard H. Jorgensen's newest book. It will motivate you to get going and to make money renovating small run-down residental properties.

This is the sequel to Jorgensen's earlier book, "Hidden Wealth in Local Real Estate." Fortunately, he has continued his unique style of grass-roots writing. The photos add realism to the topics discussed.

But in this book Jorgensen goes into greater detail than in his first book. I especially enjoyed his periodic two-line sage wisdom "advisories" throughout the book such as "Real estate investing is a form of forced savings. We're to save other people's money: the banks', the tenants', and the government's." If you don't understand that one maybe you are not destined to be a successful real estate investor.

However, don't put blind faith in everything Jorgensen suggests. For example, he spends an entire chapter extolling the virtues of the contract for deed which he says is a great way to acquire real estate with little cash. That is probably true

Book review

where Jorgensen invests in the small town of Marshall, Minn. But there are many pitfalls to this method where the seller retains the title until the buyer makes all or an agreed number of payments before receiving the deed. Incidentally, the contract for deed technique is called an agreement for sale, contract for sale, land contract, installment land sale contract, and a zillion other names in various states.

Other topics discussed in this book of common-sense advice include how to get started, success stories of everyday people, how to avoid real estate investing pitfalls, the fixer upper, how to get financing, the new tax laws, how to enhance profits, self-management and sweat equity, screening tenants, credit and collection policy, tenant problems, and how to cash in on the fruits of your labor.

Jorgensen's new book is filled with practical advice for property owners who want to be successful. With over 20 years of experience owning investment real estate, Jorgensen knows what he writes about. At times he sounds a little corny and he admits to being stingy, but the knowledge shared in this book is priceless because it works. Highly recommended for beginner real estate investors as well as experienced landlords who need to refresh and gain new insights.
Tribune Media Services

Fig. 2-6. I am honored that my book THE NO NONSENSE LANDLORD was highly recommended by Robert Bruss.

NAME AND ADDRESS OF CREDIT BUREAU MAKING REPORT

☐ SINGLE REFERENCE   ☐ IN FILE REPORT   ☐ TRADE REPORT

CREDIT BURAU OF ANYTOWN
1131 MAIN STREET
ANYTOWN, ANYSTATE 12345

☐ FULL REPORT   ☐ EMPLOY & TRADE REPORT   ☐ PREVIOUS RESIDENCE REPORT

☒ OTHER _____

	Date Received 0-0-00	CONFIDENTIAL crediscope® REPORT
FOR MASTER CARD 1234 MAIN STREET ANYTOWN, ANYSTATE 56789	Date Mailed 0-0-00	
	In File Since 0000	▣ Member Associated Credit Bureaus, Inc.
	Inquired As: 0-0-00	

REPORT ON:	LAST NAME CONSUMER	FIRST NAME ALAN	INITIAL A.	SOCIAL SECURITY NUMBER 123-45-6789	SPOUSE'S NAME SUSAN B.
ADDRESS:	CITY 1234 ANY STREET	STATE: ANYTOWN, ANYSTATE	ZIP CODE 56789	SINCE: 0000	SPOUSE'S SOCIAL SECURITY NO. 987-65-4321

COMPLETE TO HERE FOR TRADE REPORT AND SKIP TO CREDIT HISTORY

PRESENT EMPLOYER: ABC COMPANY, INC	POSITION HELD: MARKETING MANAGER	SINCE: 14 years	DATE EMPLOY VERIFIED 0-0-00	EST. MONTHLY INCOME $ 4200

COMPLETE TO HERE FOR EMPLOYMENT AND TRADE REPORT AND SKIP TO CREDIT HISTORY

DATE OF BIRTH 1951	NUMBER OF DEPENDENTS INCLUDING SELF: 3	▣ OWNS OR BUYING HOME ☐ RENTS HOME	OTHER: (EXPLAIN) ☐
FORMER ADDRESS:	CITY:	STATE:	FROM:	TO:

FORMER EMPLOYER:	POSITION HELD:	FROM:	TO:	EST. MONTHLY INCOME $

SPOUSE'S EMPLOYER: Doctor MEDICAL	POSITION HELD: Accounts Manager	SINCE: 2 years	DATE EMPLOY VERIFIED 0-0-00	EST. MONTHLY INCOME $ 1000

WHOSE	KIND OF BUSINESS AND ID CODE	DATE REPORTED AND METHOD OF REPORTING	DATE OPENED	DATE OF LAST PAYMENT	HIGHEST CREDIT OR LAST CONTRACT	PRESENT STATUS BALANCE OWING	PAST DUE AMOUNT	NO. OF PAYMENTS	NO. MONTHS HISTORY REVIEWED	30-59 DAYS ONLY	60-89 DAYS ONLY	90 DAYS AND OVER	TYPE & TERMS (MANNER OF PAYMENT)	REMARKS
J	Am Exp	Auto	0-00	0-00	$640	0	0	12	12	0	0	0	Revolving	
J	Sta Oil	Auto	0-00	0-00	$160	0	0	12	12	0	0	0	Revolving	
J	JCPen	Auto	0-00	0-00	$110	0	0	12	12	0	0	0	Revolving	
J	Dayt H	Auto	0-00	0-00	$380	0	0	12	12	0	0	0	Revolving	
J	Sears	Auto	0-00	0-00	$1400	$600	0	12	12	0	0	0	Installment $100 mo	
	Bank	Manual	0-00	0-00	$12000	$4000	0	36	20	0	0	0	Installment $388 mo	
	Real Es	Manual	0-00	0-00	$76000	$64000	0	30y	34	0	0	0	Installment $580 mo	

Bank reports: Maintains two personal checking accounts with medium 4 figure balance no
record of any over-draft. Also joint savings account with high 5 figure
balance.

COURT RECORDS: Nothing on file.

Fig. 2-7. A good credit record and report can open most financial doors.

Good credit will buy good investments

I told Mark and Sue once they got their real estate education they should start looking for properties in their home community.

I reviewed their income and financial status and from this determined that a duplex in the $120,000 price range would be a good starter investment. They had a down payment, either by using their savings or borrowing against their savings. The payment on a 25-year mortgage at $11\frac{1}{2}$ percent interest on the remaining $100,000 would be $997.08 a month. I figured the taxes on this property would be $200 a month and insurance about $45 a month. A duplex in this price range should bring $650 to $700 a month income per unit. The payment, insurance, taxes, and interest would be $1242.08 with $1300 to $1400 a month income. A good unit would require no costly maintenance at first. This meant the property would have a positive cash flow. In addition they could deduct $1090.81 per year from their personal income from depreciation on a $120,000 investment.

All this was readily available to this young couple because they had a good credit rating and this made investments readily available to them. Their credit report is shown in Fig. 2-7.

3

How to Apply for Credit

BORROWING MONEY CAN BE AN ANXIOUS TIME. SOMETIMES THE ANXIETY LEVEL is increased because we wait until the last minute to make a purchase and then rush to the bank for a loan with no plans. I suppose it is human nature, and it is certainly a part of our impulse-buying society. We see a new car or a new boat and we want it right now. Or we may be in debt over our heads and need some quick cash to stay out of serious financial trouble. And there are times when no matter how well we plan and how hard we try to live within our budget, an emergency arises and there is a need for money immediately.

Is the loan necessary?

Knowing why a loan is necessary, whether it is for a car, household furniture, a home, vacation, or whatever is probably the first question to ask. Do you really need, and can you afford, what you are buying? It's only common sense to have an answer to these questions—answers that make financial sense.

Most of us don't just go out at random and borrow money. It is a matter of knowing what we are doing and why we need the money. But more important it is a matter of being prepared. And being prepared certainly can lessen the personal anxiety.

It's certainly not all that easy to borrow money, whether it is for an emergency, necessity, or luxury. But borrowing is important and necessary and is certainly an acceptable way to acquire money.

The point is that we all have to borrow money at times. Why we need the money is another story which depends entirely on personal choices and priorities, such as:

- a new home
- home remodeling
- a recreational home or vehicle
- college tuition and expenses
- vacations
- weddings
- pay bills
- furniture and household goods
- cars

The list could go on endlessly.

Am I buying smart?

Once you know why you want and need the money, the next question is, "Do I really need what I am buying, and if so, can I afford it?"

The answer to this question takes a little more planning if you want to avoid severe anxieties. The foremost cause of credit and financial distress for most people is buying something they don't need and can't afford. Let me repeat:

> The number one cause of financial trouble and failure is overbuying and overspending—buying something you don't need and can't afford.

Think it over, Am I buying smart?

If you've decided that you have made the right decision, the next step is getting the loan. Ask yourself this question:

> "How much do I need to borrow, when do I need it, and how can I pay it back?"

How much you need may be more than you had originally planned. There are always hidden or extra costs that creep in that you don't count on. For instance, take the case of buying a new car. If there is a trade-in and a purchase price of $5,000 after the trade-in, keep in mind that any previous loan has to be paid off. Also, expect to pay sales tax, license fees, and insurance.

Or, in the case of buying a home, there are considerable hidden costs. There are points to pay for the privilege of borrowing from the bank. In addition, there are attorney fees, appraisal fees, realtor fees, deed, and mortgage taxes. It is also important to know how much the payment is going to be. A $75,000 house loan over 25 years at 10% interest is $670.88. A $95,000 house loan over 25 years at 10% is $849.77. A $150,000 house loan over 25 years at 10% is $1341.75. The loaning institution in all likelihood will ask for an escrow payment which includes taxes and insurance and this can add another $200 to $400 onto the payment.

Next, know how that loan payment will fit into your budget. For instance if most of your payments are due on the first of the month you might want to consider having this new loan payment due on the 15th. Then there isn't such a strain on the cash at the first of each month.

Finding the right banker

The next step is finding a loaning institution of good repute that will best serve your needs. If you have a good credit rating you are in the drivers seat and can pick and choose the bank you want to do business with. With a good rating they all will want to do business with you.

The following agencies have available personal, car, furniture and home loans:

- Banks
- Small Business Administration
- Federal Housing Administration
- Farmers Home Administration
- Housing and Urban Development
- Savings and Loan Associations
- Leasing Companies
- Finance and Small Loan Companies
- Private and Government Credit Unions
- Consumer Loan Companies

For open account credit:

- Most Major Department Stores
- Credit Card Companies

Specialty firms financing their own products:

- General Motors Acceptance Corporation
- Chrysler Credit Corporation
- Ford Motor Credit Corporation
- General Electric Credit Corporation
- Whirlpool Acceptance Corporation

Here the merchant can sell the product and get financing through the respective manufacturing company—a General Electric Appliance dealer can get financing through General Electric Credit Corporation. Ask the dealer where you do business.

There are some good financing bargains if you shop around. Car companies are now offering financing for 2.9% and even for 0% interest. The car companies are interested in selling cars and not in making profits on financing. When you realize the price we pay for cars now, it's certainly understandable why they want to sell them and why there is plenty of profit built in.

Small loan companies specialize in providing financing for consolidation loans and household furniture loans. They deal with a high-risk clientele—those with credit discrepancies, low-paying jobs, or those who have less of an ability to repay. Consequently these companies charge a higher rate of interest because they know in the long run there's a higher loss ratio.

What about a credit union?

A credit union is considered to be a not-for-profit bank—a bank owned by the people that use it. Credit unions are usually organized by a group of employees specifically to serve that group—government employees, unions, teachers, and some private companies have their own credit unions. If you work for any branch of the government there are credit unions serving you. There are about 15,000 credit unions throughout the country. Credit unions usually have complete banking services, which include savings, checking, loans, and mortgages. There are some credit unions that have their own credit cards.

One benefit of doing business with a credit union is that many times they can provide the same services at a lower rate of interest and without the complications and inconvenience of banks. Usually their payment is taken right out of your paycheck each month so that they don't have to worry about delinquent payments. Most of the time their interest rates are lower and their checking accounts less expensive than a traditional bank.

Credit is not limited to banks, loaning agencies, and credit unions. In fact, there is really no limit to the availability of credit. The largest bank in the country down to the small corner drug store where you live offer credit nowadays.

What kinds of credit are available?

Not only are there all kinds of loaning institutions but there are different types of credit and loans. Let's take a look.

Open account credit   Open account credit allows you to charge today and pay at the end of the month. As you are paying off the bill you can charge additionally along the way. Open account credit includes the small corner drug store, your clothing store and similar types of merchants, as well as the dentist and doctor.

Installment loans   Installment loans are paid on the basis of equal monthly payments over an extended period of time. Usually installment loans include loans for appliances, furniture, vacations, vacation homes, cars, and recreational vehicles.

30-day charge account   With a 30-day charge account you can buy merchandise on the spot and use it free for 30 days. In 30 days the payment is due in full and usually there is no interest charged.

Revolving charge   This is similar to the 30-day charge account and the open account credit. However, a revolving account means the account is not due in full in 30 days. It can be set up on a monthly plan that you agree to. However, there is usually a 15 to 20 percent interest charge for a revolving account.

Home equity loan   Banks recently started promoting home equity loans. Here is how they work. Let's say you own a home valued at $75,000 with a $50,000 mortgage balance. This represents $25,000 equity. Banks will use this equity as security on a loan up to 80 percent of that equity. Eighty percent of $25,000 is $10,000 which banks will lend.

Banks charge about 1½ percent interest above the current real estate mortgage interest rate and will demand payment 12 years from the time of the mortgage. In some cases there is an application fee to process the loan of up to $100. There is also a mortgage tax fee, a filing fee, and a title search fee.

The money borrowed can be used for anything—a car, vacation, investments, or a higher standard of living. One advantage of a home equity loan is that the interest can be deducted on your income tax. One disadvantage of a home equity loan is that if you fall behind on the payments your home is subject to foreclosure. With a home equity loan you can borrow one lump sum or you can borrow as much as you wish on a check by check basis.

Home mortgage   The home mortgage is simply that—the availability of a loan through a bank or savings and loan to buy a personal home.

There are some tips regarding a home mortgage that ought to be considered. For instance, there are some considerable expenses in getting a home mortgage that often are not mentioned until the deal has been completed. These costs include:

- Points
- Down Payment
- Attorney Fee for Title Opinion
- Deed Preparation
- Appraisal Fee
- Title Search
- Title Registration
- Mortgage Tax
- Credit Report

Of these most are self explanatory with the exception of points, so let's talk about them in greater detail.

Do you know why banks charge points? For one reason, and one reason alone. Profit. There is no firm, sound reason for points being paid to banks other than pure unadulterated greed.

Do you know what the banks will tell you if you ask why you pay points? They will say that it's for the cost of processing the loan application. That's bull. Interest paid to the bank covers the work they do in processing loans. Interest is what banks charge to pay the cost of operating the bank and making a profit.

Points are simply for more profit. I have a feeling that if some consumer group took this up as a cause, changes could and would take place.

Real-estate investment loans   Buying investment real estate is a sure way to accumulate wealth and financial security. In fact, I don't know of any better way for the average person to accumulate this kind of money.

Getting a loan for real estate investments is a matter of searching out the sources. Most banks demand a 20 percent down payment for investment loans. In addition they will charge an extra $1^{1}/_{2}$ to 2 percent interest on investment property.

The best place to look for real estate investment financing is through a former owner or the seller. With the right negotiations you can end up paying a small down payment and a lower rate of interest than through loaning institutions. This is called a contract for deed sale and mortgage. The one thing to be concerned about in a contract for deed is that the holder of that contract can repossess the property if you are delinquent only one payment.

Business loan   The Small Business Administration (SBA) have two types of loans available to small businesses. One is a direct loan from the SBA. In order to qualify for a direct loan you must have been turned down by two traditional loaning agencies, in writing. I've been told it is not difficult to acquire these two letters of non-acceptance.

The second type of an SBA loan is a participation loan with the bank. The bank loans out the money and the SBA guarantees the loan. That means that if you default on the loan the SBA will pay off the bank. SBA direct loans are usually two percent less interest than a traditional bank loan.

There is one more option for a business loan—a lease buy back loan. If you own equipment, computers, trucks, or whatever and if the equipment is all paid for, a leasing company will buy the equipment and lease it back to you. They charge interest, and at the end of the lease you will have a buy back provision.

Pawn shop   The last resort is a pawn shop. Pawn shops will take your property, hold it for a certain period of time, giving you the right to pay off the loan and get the property back. If you do not return they have the right to sell the property. Usually the pawn shop will borrow at a small percentage of the value of the property and the interest they charge is high.

The personal loan application

The next step in processing a loan is filling out the application itself. It's fairly universal and simple. An example of a loan application for a standard bank loan is shown in Fig. 3-1.

Figure 3-2 is a loan application from an appliance dealer. The financing will be done through the company and the company will have recourse to the dealer if the purchaser doesn't make the payments. Usually on this kind of application a great deal of information is not requested because the loan is basically guaranteed by the dealer. About the only thing the company does is call for a credit report. If there's a record of good pay the loan is almost instantly and automatically approved.

Personal
Financial Statement

To: _____

If I have any questions regarding the completion of this form, I should contact my representative at the bank.

I may apply for a credit extension, loan or other financial accommodation alone or together with someone else, ("co-applicant"). If I apply with a co-applicant and our combined assets and debts can meaningfully and fairly be presented together, the co-applicant and I may complete this required statement and any supporting schedules jointly. Otherwise, separate forms and schedules are required.

APPLICANT

Name _____ *Social Security number* _____

Address _____

Telephone number _____ *Date of birth* _____

Present employer _____ *Position* _____

Address _____

Business phone _____ *Loan purpose* _____

CO-APPLICANT

Name _____ *Social Security number* _____

Address _____

Telephone number _____ *Date of birth* _____

Present employer _____ *Position* _____

Address _____

Business phone _____ *Loan purpose* _____

Fig. 3-1. This is a copy of a standard credit application used by most banks and loaning institutions.

Date of valuation

● Round all amounts to the nearest $100
● Attach separate sheet if you need more space to complete detail schedule

Assets (assets you own)	Amount	Liabilities (debts you owe)	Amount
Cash in this bank: Checking		Loans payable to banks (schedule 7)	
Savings		Loans payable to others (schedule 7)	
C.D.s		Installment contracts payable (schedule 7)	
IRA		Amounts due to dept. stores and others	
Cash in other banks		Credit cards (MasterCard, Visa & others)	
Due from friends, relatives and others (schedule 1)		Income taxes payable	
Mortgage and contracts for deed owned (schedule 2)		Other taxes payable	
Securities owned (schedule 3)			
Cash surrender value of life insurance (schedule 4)		Loans on life insurance (schedule 4)	
Homestead (schedule 5)			
Other real estate owned (schedule 5)		Mortgage on homestead (schedule 6)	
Automobiles (year, make, model)		Mortgage or liens on other real estate owned (schedule 6)	
		Contracts for deed (schedule 6)	
Personal property			
		Other liabilities (detail)	
Other assets (detail)			
		TOTAL LIABILITIES	
		Net worth (total assets less total liabilities)	
TOTAL		TOTAL	

Annual income	Applicant	Co-applicant	Contingent liabilities	Amount
Salary			As endorser	
Commissions			As guarantor	
Dividends			Lawsuits	
Interest			For taxes	
Rentals			Other (detail)	
Alimony, child support or maintenance (you need not show this unless you wish us to consider it).				
Other				
			☐ Check here if "none"	
TOTAL INCOME			TOTAL CONTINGENT LIABILITIES	

SCHEDULE 1 DUE FROM FRIENDS, RELATIVES AND OTHERS

Name of debtor	Owed to	Collateral	How payable	Maturity date	Unpaid balance
			$ per		
			$ per		
			$ per		
			TOTAL		

SCHEDULE 2 MORTGAGE AND CONTRACTS FOR DEED OWNED

Name of debtor	Type of property	1st or 2nd lien	Owed to	How payable	Unpaid balance
				$ per	
				$ per	
				$ per	
				$ per	
				TOTAL	

Fig. 3-1. Continued.

SCHEDULE 3 SECURITIES OWNED

No. shares or Bond amount	Description	In whose name(s) registered	Cost	Present Market value	L-listed U-unlisted
		TOTAL			

SCHEDULE 4 LIFE INSURANCE

Insured	Insurance company	Beneficiary	Face value of policy	Cash value	Loans
			TOTAL		

SCHEDULE 5 REAL ESTATE

Address and type of property	Title in name(s) of	Monthly Income	Cost Year acquired	Present Market value	Amount of Insurance
Homestead			$ .... Year		
			$ .... Year		
			$ .... Year		
			$ .... Year		
			$ .... Year		

SCHEDULE 6 MORTGAGES OR LIENS ON REAL ESTATE

To whom payable	How payable	Interest Rate	Maturity Date	Unpaid Balance
Homestead	$ per			
	$ per			
	$ per			
	$ per			
	$ per			

SCHEDULE 7 LOANS PAYABLE TO BANKS & OTHERS AND INSTALLMENT CONTRACTS PAYABLE

To whom payable	Address	Collateral or Unsecured	How payable	Maturity Date	Unpaid Balance
			$ per		
			$ per		
			$ per		
			$ per		
			$ per		
			$ per		
			$ per		
			$ per		

Fig. 3-1. Continued.

	APPLICANT		CO-APPLICANT	
	Yes No		Yes No	

Have I ever gone through bankruptcy or had a judgment against me?

☐ Yes   ☐ No   ☐ Yes   ☐ No

Are any assets pledged or debts secured except as shown?

☐ Yes   ☐ No   ☐ Yes   ☐ No

Have I made a will?

☐ Yes   ☐ No   ☐ Yes   ☐ No

Number of dependents
(if none, check "None")

_____ ☐ None   _____ ☐ None

Marital status (answer only if this financial statement is provided in connection with a request for secured credit or applicant is seeking a joint account with spouse.)

☐ Married   ☐ Married
☐ Separated   ☐ Separated
☐ Unmarried   ☐ Unmarried

(Unmarried includes single, divorced, widowed)

The foregoing statement, submitted for the purpose of obtaining credit, is true and correct in every detail and fairly shows my/our financial condition at the time indicated. I/we will give you prompt written notice of any subsequent substantial change in such financial condition occurring before discharge of my/our obligations to you. I/we understand that you will retain this personal financial statement whether or not you approve the credit in connection with which it is submitted. You are authorized to check my/our credit and employment history or any other information contained herein.

THE UNDERSIGNED CERTIFY THAT THE INFORMATION CONTAINED ON THIS FORM HAS BEEN CAREFULLY REVIEWED AND THAT IT IS TRUE AND CORRECT IN ALL RESPECTS.

_____   _____
Date   My signature

_____   _____
Date   Co-applicant signature (if you are requesting the financial accommodation jointly)

Fig. 3-1. Continued.

In addition to the loan application itself there is a list of terms of the contract that the buyer must sign. These terms are often in small print and bear scrutiny. Here is a list of some standard terms of most dealer contracts and appliance loan applications:

- Finance Charge
  Most dealer contracts and appliance contracts charge 18 percent.
- Minimum Monthly Payment
- Security
  Covers the merchandise, appliance purchased.
- Filing Fees
  A fee charged to file the document with public register of deeds. This fee is usually paid by the buyer.

Please read the following before completing this form: (1) Applicant represents that the information given in this application is complete and accurate and authorizes us to check with credit reporting agencies, credit references and other sources disclosed herein in investigating the information given. (2) Applicant requests a credit card if our current consumer credit plan provides for the issuance of such a card. (3) Married applicants may apply for an individual account. READ AND SIGN THE ATTACHED AGREEMENT BEFORE SUBMITTING YOUR APPLICATION.

1. TELL US ABOUT YOURSELF

PLEASE PRINT

First Name	Middle Initial	Last Name		

Present Address

City			State	Zip Code

Previous Address (if less than two years at present address)	City	State	Zip Code

Birthdate / /	Social Security No.	Home Phone No. ( )	Business Phone No. ( )

Employer	How Long (Years)	Annual Income* $	Occupation: (✔)

No. Dependents	○ Own ○ Board	How Long (Years)	Mortgage/Rent Payment	Occupation:

1. ○ Professional/ Technical   4. ○ Self-Employed
2. ○ Sales   5. ○ Retired
3. ○ Clerical   6. ○ Other

○ Rent   ○ Live with Relatives   Mortgage/Rent Payment $

Credit References: (✔)
○ Checking   ○ Savings   ○ VISA   ○ MasterCard   ○ Sears/ Discover   ○ American Express/ Optima   ○ Dept. Stores

2. PLEASE COMPLETE FOR CO-APPLICANT OR AUTHORIZED USER

Co-Applicant must sign Section 4 (Acknowledgement Signatures).

First Name	Middle Initial	Last Name		

Present Address	City	State	Zip Code

Annual Income*	Social Security No.	Relationship to Applicant ○ Spouse ○ Other	If individual listed above is Co-Applicant, check circle. ○

3. INSURANCE OPTIONS

Indicate coverage chosen by signing and completing one of the following options. If insurance is not elected, do not sign or complete the following options.

By signing below, you acknowledge for any insurance elected that: (1) the purchase of such insurance was voluntary and was not required by us in the extension of credit; (2) the decision to purchase such insurance was made after we disclosed the cost of the insurance as set out in the agreement; and (3) you may obtain property insurance from a person of your own choosing other than us.

Single Credit Life and Accountholder Disability Insurance with Property Insurance   ○ is elected (62)   ○ is not elected

Joint Credit Life and Accountholder Disability Insurance with Property Insurance   ○ is elected (42)   ○ is not elected

X

Buyer's Signature	Date	Age	If joint elected, complete name of Co-Buyer	Age

Fig. 3-2. This is an application from a national appliance finance corporation.

- Default
  At time of default the company has the right to demand the entire unpaid balance.
  At time of default the company can repossess the merchandise, resell the property and then collect any remaining balance.
- Credit
  This gives the company the right to investigate your credit capacity and credit history.
- Insurance Options
  Insurance is not required. However, there are companies who give the option to buy coverage so that if you suffer disability or death the loan will be paid off by the insurance company.

Although most loaning agencies and banks are ethical and trustworthy it still pays to take time and know what you are doing before signing any document.

After all, you are entering into an agreement that has great bearing on your credit and financial life. Check this list:

- Is this a reputable firm?
- Can the salesperson be trusted?
- Don't be pushed into signing any document that the salesperson will hold for 24 hours.
- If the contract is different than what the salesperson represented, get that difference straightened out before signing anything.
- Don't let the company or the salesperson change the contract once the deal is made.
- Don't depend on a verbal agreement or promises. Get it in writing.
- If there are blank spaces on the application form be sure they are lined out and cannot be filled in after you have signed.
- Read all the print and this includes the fine print.

Here are some additional tips about buying: If you are dealing with home improvement firms like roofing, basement sealing, siding, and other repair services, know who you are dealing with. Check them out closely, especially if they are not local. There is hardly a newscast where some slick salesperson or con artist hasn't taken someone.

As a matter of fact, I would never do business with an out of town business firm if that same service or product is available locally. The chances of being taken are too great. When in doubt, one can always ask this question

"What happens if I have trouble? Who will help me then?"

Student loans

The cost of education is a primary concern of every family in America. The reason for this concern is that it costs $18,000 a year for a student to go to a public college or university. The cost for a private college or university can exceed $45,000 per year.

The cost of course is of concern, but how to pay for this education is of greater concern. Many families really don't know where or how to get financing for their children. Most of us don't have that kind of money in reserve. We've spent the money raising the family and just haven't had the ability to put aside enough for college. Raising a family is no small financial chore in itself. However, there is a way. In our credit society there are various opportunities for students to acquire financial aid for a college education.

There are basically three different ways to finance a college education. Well, there are four, if you consider paying for it on your own. But for the average person that money isn't available so there are three methods, as follows:

1. Grant. A grant is an outright gift and can come from a college or a governmental agency. Check with your college or university.

2. Work Study. This means the college will provide the student with an on-campus job and they can work their way through school. Again, check with the college and university.

3. Direct Loan. A direct loan is money borrowed from a loaning institution and is guaranteed by the federal government.

Guaranteed student loans

A guaranteed student loan is just like any other bank loan except it is guaranteed by the federal government. As long as the student remains at least half-time in school the loan does not have to be paid back. However, once the student leaves school, quits or graduates, there is a short grace period and then payments must be made.

To qualify for a guaranteed student loan the student must be accepted and enrolled in an eligible institution of higher education, and must be classified as at least a half-time student.

The student's family must have an adjusted gross income of $30,000 or less.

The maximum of a guaranteed student loan is $2,500 per year for an undergraduate with a maximum of $12,500, and $5,000 per year for a graduate student with a $25,000 maximum. Students apply for their loan through any participating financial institution—usually your local bank.

That student loan is guaranteed by the government. As long as the student remains in school the loan does not have to be paid back but once the student leaves school this obligation, as with any other obligation, must be paid back. If not it becomes a derogatory part of the student's credit history.

For further information regarding student loans contact the loan office at the college or university. For additional information contact:

Federal Student Aid Information Center
1-800-333-4636

or write:

Department of Education
Washington, DC, 20202.

Ask for their excellent brochure titled:

"Financial Aid from the U.S. Department of Education"

This is an 81-page booklet, well done, with complete details regarding all types of student loans.

With degree in hand what is next?

During the four years it takes to get a college education students will have taken a number of loans which means at the end of four years there could be a number of payments, in which case a good consideration is a consolidation loan.

A consolidation loan is designed to combine all the loan debts into one single new loan and one payment. Under this plan any of the following loans will qualify for this consolidation:

- Guaranteed Student Loan
- Federally Insured Student Loans
- Auxiliary Loans to Assist Students
- Supplemental Loans for Students
- National Direct/Defense Student Loans
- Perkins Loans
- Health Profession Student Loans

To qualify for a consolidation loan the student must:

- Have an outstanding debt of at least $5,000
- Not be delinquent or in default on any of the loans

The repayment plan for a consolidation loan is from 10 to 25 years; $5,000—10 years, $45,000—up to 25 years.

Interest on a consolidation loan is at the average rate of all the combine loans, but not less than nine percent.

For further information here is a list of those places that can help. Write to the Higher Education Assistance Foundation with offices located at:

Suite 600, 6800 College Blvd.
Overland Park, KS 66211
(913-345-1300)

10-23 15th Street NW, Suite 1000
Washington, DC 20005
(202-289-4720)

85 East 7th Place, Suite 500
St. Paul, MN 55101
(612-227-7661)

Cornhusker Bank, Suite 304
Lincoln, NE 68521
(402-476-9129)

1912 Capital Ave.
Suite 320
Cheyenne, WY 82001
(307-635-3259)

Union Building, Suite 900
723 Kanawha Blvd.
Charleston, WV 25301
(304-345-7211)

404 James Robertson Parkway
Parkway Towers, Suite 1802
Nashville, TN 37219
(615-255-2470)

There is a federally chartered, stockholder-owned (New York Stock Exchange) corporation called Sallie Mae which provides financial services to educational institutions. This includes buying insured student loans for consolidation. Here is their address for additional information:

Sallie Mae
Smart Loan Account
1050 Thomas Jefferson Street NW
Washington, DC 20007
(1-800-524-9100)

4

Business and Personal Loans

THERE WAS A TIME, AND NOT TOO LONG AGO, WHEN BANKS MADE US ALL SHIRK when we applied for a loan. Sometimes we were made to feel downright stupid because we had to borrow money. It was, at times, almost a humiliating experience.

Changing times have changed the banking business

Back then when we were accepted for a loan, at any bank, that's all that mattered. The next time we needed money it was a matter of returning humbly to the same bank and meekly applying for another loan. If the payments on the loan were made as agreed the bank usually accepted that and there was no hassle, no trouble, and a new loan was approved. That is how most of us established our banking relationship.

The thought of negotiating any of the terms of the loan was unheard of and so remote it wasn't even considered. The banker basically laid out the terms, the interest, the security, and the payment plan, and that's the way it was, take it or leave it. We simply needed the money and figured, "The money is available, they've approved the loan, and that's good enough for me."

Things have changed dramatically since then. Now you have the upper hand when it comes to dealing with a banker. You can control your own destiny in the banking world and there's no longer any need to be intimidated, and it's certainly not necessary to beg or grovel. You are *their* customer paying for *their* services and have a right to be treated with due respect and consideration.

That being the case, let's look and see what we can expect from our modern day banker and how we can negotiate the terms.

What is our friendly banker up to?

First, let's discuss what a banker does. For one thing, the banker makes money and plenty of it. If you don't believe that, take another look at some of those bank buildings built with our money.

Can it be said that profit is their only motive? I suppose it's safe to say that profit is their primary motive, however, banks do provide a public service in which we all participate, and that is that they make money available to everyone.

How then do you get this money? It takes some doing on your part but the primary concern is that you make an impression with a banker.

Why and when do we need the banker?

Before you make that impression on the banker, however, let's find out just why we need his services.

The bank—and when I speak of banks, I include savings and loans, credit unions, loaning agencies, and all of the institutions that loan money—is the primary source of almost all of our credit buying. Credit buying consists of financing a car, our home, establishing a checking account, a credit card, and almost all financial needs. You would be hard pressed to buy anything on a credit basis if it wasn't for bankers.

Who has the right to use the bank, who should use the bank, and who should apply for a bank loan? The answer to this covers about everyone that needs financial aid. Bankers in general are friendly and accommodating people and are available to meet your financial needs. The bank will lend to anyone who is willing to pay their obligations. Any person who meets their requirements—primarily that of having the ability to repay the loan—is eligible for a bank loan.

When is the right time to get a bank loan? The obvious answer is when there is a need for financial aid. But more important, the right time is when you feel secure about paying back that obligation, whether it's for a car, home, vacation, or personal home.

A factor to consider before buying a home is location. If you have a job that involves moving periodically it may not be a good time to invest in a home. On the other hand, if it looks like you're settled in one community and the future looks bright for your company and business then it is a time to invest in a home, expand a business operation, or buy investment property—if all else is satisfactory.

Preparing for the loan

As stated before, one of the primary concerns you should have when you start out to get a loan is making an impression on the banker. Now, if you really want to get the banker's attention and make an impression, walk into the bank with a $50,000 savings certificate and apply for a $5,000 loan. This will not only get his attention but will get first class service and a loan quickly and easily. In fact, the banker will probably jump through hoops to get your business. Of course, if we had a $50,000 savings certificate we probably wouldn't need a $5,000 loan.

You and I know the $50,000 savings doesn't represent a person who needs to borrow and make monthly payments. Most people don't have $50,000—or $5,000 for that matter. That's why we're at the bank. So, if you don't have the $50,000 and need a loan, what is the next best way to impress your banker? The answer is simple, and every banker will tell you: Have a good credit record. Good credit may not be $50,000 but it is as good a second best as there is, and it will definitely make it a lot easier to get the banker's attention, make an impression, and ultimately get the loan.

With good credit you can negotiate the terms

Not only will good credit get the banker's attention but it will place you in a position of being able to negotiate the terms of the loan. Let's take a look at them.

Interest Banks borrow money on the basis of the Federal Discount Rate. They also use our savings for loans. They add several percentage points to the money and this is what they charge us for interest. For instance, the bank may pay six percent for the money they borrow and then charge us 10 to 11 percent for the loan.

Interest rates can vary from bank to bank, small loan companies, credit unions, savings and loan institutions, and credit card companies. That's why it's a good idea to shop around.

How much we provide for collateral and security can also affect the interest the bank will charge. For instance, if we can offer the bank a savings account as security the bank most likely will give a better rate of interest than they will on, let's say, a used car. Those who have a $50,000 savings account can probably get a loan on their signature and with the lowest rate of interest the bank has to offer. I've heard General Motors has enough borrowing power that they can borrow millions of dollars as a much lower rate than you and I could.

Security Security is another negotiable factor in getting a loan. What the bank needs and wants (and they usually want everything they can get their hands on) can depend on our credit history, our income, and our earning power.

With good earning power and good credit in your favor, it's best to point this out to the banker and subsequently not have to give as much security.

Insurance Bankers will push insurance on loans because it is a high profit item. Loan agencies will use highly emotional terms when making their sales pitch for insurance, such as "your family, your health, your loved ones, and your savings should all be protected." They will often ask, "What if something happens and you can't meet the payments?" They insist that the only reason for the insurance is to protect against those things that could cause a financial hardship, and they may be right. However, the bankers are in this business for one reason and one reason alone—to make money.

Insurance at most banks is high-priced. Therefore, before agreeing to their policy and terms, check with other agencies. You don't have to buy the bank insurance simply because you get their loan.

There's no doubt about it, we do need insurance—auto insurance, home owner's insurance, and life insurance. But there are some policies like health and disability that is high-priced and not essential. Check the policies you have and there could already be adequate coverage.

Impress your banker with a plan of action

The best way to get along with a banker is to have a well-established loan plan. There may be some apprehension about the time we make contact with the banker so it is best to be prepared. Don't hesitate to discuss the plan with the banker.

Here is a list of some of the things bankers will be looking for that should be included in the plan:

- Occupation. Provide a complete description of your job or business status, what your future expectations are, and how you believe progress is going.

- Biography. This includes a general history of your life, college degrees, titles, honors, and civic activities. Most bankers are community-oriented people and they like others who are so involved.

- Professional Advisors. Give the names and addresses of your attorney, accountant, and any other professional service used in your business affairs.

- Income Tax Returns. Having two years' tax returns are beneficial.

What does the banker want to know

Each and every bank or loan agency is going to want a considerable amount of information about your financial and business record. Here's a list the banker will be looking at:

- Ability to Pay. Probably the most important factor a loaning agency will be looking for is whether there is a record of secure and steady employment with adequate income. This income must be sufficient to cover living expenses, payment on debts, and the loan payment.

- List of Living Expenses. This will include current payments for utilities, heat, taxes, car payments, house payments, and normal everyday bills and obligations. The loaning agency will determine from this information whether another payment can be handled before approving the loan.

- Amount of Money Owed. This includes bank loans, car loans, house mortgage, credit card balances, and open account balances. This will determine if there is any equity or security for the loan. This is net worth.

- Willingness to Pay. This really gets down to the nitty-gritty of the loan approval. The bank is going to check credit history. This information will be acquired from a credit reporting agency. The information of course will include how you pay your bills. To make a strong impression on the banker make certain your credit file and credit information is in good order and there's a history of good paying habits. (NOTE: In doing the research on this book a banker told me that if they see even the slightest blemish on a credit history the red flag goes up and the loan is then scrutinized with extreme care.)
- A List of Assets and Liabilities. This list will include all property owned and the equity in that property. Equity, the difference between the value of property and the mortgage on the property, represents security and collateral. Security and collateral impresses bankers.
- Personal History. The banker will want to know how stable and reliable you are which includes how long at present address. If there is a history of moving from job to job and community to community the chances of impressing the banker and getting a loan is questionable.

That covers the material needed for a loan. Most of us buy and borrow on the spur of the moment. We see something we like and we want it—right now. Even so, it's best to have some sort of preparation so the banker knows what to expect.

Applying for a small business loan

A business loan, no matter what size, is a big step for almost every small business. Because of its importance—and that importance can be the difference between success and failure—there should be a great deal of time and thought spent on the preparation of the loan. The first stop toward that goal, that of getting the loan, is to make a positive impression on the banker.

The first question to be answered is: "Why is the loan necessary?"

As we all know, good deals come along all the time. Most of us who are the entrepreneurial types know that it's human nature for us to go for that good deal. The trouble with trying to close that good deal is that things need our immediate attention and this means moving on the project right now. It's a matter of making some quick decisions and taking quick action. There is certainly nothing the matter with doing business on this basis; in fact, that's really what has made our free enterprise system work. At any rate, that good deal could be for new equipment, a new building, expansion of the present business through growth, or the acquisition of another entire business. Consequently it does take some steps to get things done quickly.

Even though most good-deal decisions mean quick action, it's important to consider plans. This is a time when there should be a well laid out plan of action for every phase of that business expansion, acquisition, or whatever.

Preparation means complete details

Actually a business loan is not that much different than a personal loan. It's a matter of providing more information in detail about the business. The best way to make a positive impression on the banker is to have a well laid out plan that includes the following information:

- How much money is needed
- What the loan is for
- How the money will benefit the business
- How the loan makes sense
- How will repayment be made

In addition the banker will want to know the following:

- Description of the business
- Old and new markets
- Competition
- Management and personnel status
- Sources of funding
- Balance sheet
- Income projections
- Current cash flow

If the loan is for purchasing a buy-out, the bank will want to know:

- History of the take-over business
- Why the owner is selling
- Determining factors for the purchase price
- Future expectations and sales
- What you can add to the business

Prepare a complete financial statement which includes both personal and business history along with a complete business financial balance sheet. An accountant may be needed to prepare some of the information.

I can't emphasize how important a well laid out plan is. This plan can literally make the difference between growth and survival. Business failures and bankruptcies dominate the business scene. Most business statisticians tell us that about one out of every 10 new businesses survive. That's why a good plan is important.

Included in the plan should be a meeting with the banker. He most likely has been around for a long time and is in a good position to know what can work and what can't. He can point out weaknesses that your over-enthusiasm might have overlooked.

From your plans, if they are well prepared, that banker can determine how the loan can be set up, how the entire business project can be carried out to an end result—that of paying off the loan as agreed. Remember, your success is also the banker's success.

Bankers will tell you that the number one cause of personal and business failure can be attributed to the lack of a viable well organized plan. And that plan must include a spending policy. Most failed businesses have virtually jumped into something they didn't know enough about, didn't get organized, and then depended totally on luck to carry them through. That's not enough, and definitely not enough for a banker. That's just not the way things work.

Additional tips that can help impress the banker

- Prepare a sound reason for the loan and a blueprint of the future. The banker wants to know if you know what you are doing.
- Bankers like numbers—but they want honest numbers. Have a well-prepared financial statement.
- Don't over-sell the report. For instance, if the business has consistently shown a 10 percent growth year after year and then you come in with a report showing an anticipated 30 percent growth, that's over-sell. The banker can see, and all this does is lose your credibility.
- Report on the future prospects of the operation and what promotions can be used to enhance the business.
- Describe any potential salary increases—especially your own.
- Point out any increases in operational costs.
- Let the banker know all about yourself. Give your personal history—with enthusiasm. Now's the time to blow your horn.
- The banker will expect both the owner and the business, and I emphasize both, to have a good credit history and pay record.

Honesty is the best policy

Do you want to know how to make your banker sick and throw up? Just lie to him and that will do it.

There is nothing more infuriating to a banker than to process a loan application and then find that the facts were, let's say, misrepresented. If that banker calls for a credit report and finds that the facts have not been totally presented, if there's a record of slovenly credit habits or if there are debts that have not been reported on the application, these things will definitely raise the hair on the back of his neck—especially if you've told him differently. And believe me, he will check your facts. He will order a complete credit investigation.

Bankers don't like surprises, especially financial exaggerations. Be honest. If it is good news or bad news, tell it like it is. If you are having financial difficulties, tell the truth about whatever problem you are having. This may enhance the chances of getting a loan much better than going through a pack of lies.

If you are dealing with a total out-and-out disastrous situation this is a time when you are probably more in need of help than at any other time in your business career. This is a time when that banker can be of help and give much needed advice. You may not get a loan but you may get a possible solution to your problems.

Usually at a time of financial crisis we become frightened—and rightfully so. There is nothing more harsh than the feeling of insecurity over the possibility of a business failure. We sometimes don't know what to do nor who to turn to. That banker might be just the person.

Listen. That banker is well-educated and well-trained. They know what they are doing, if not, they would not be in the position they are in. In general I think bankers can be trusted.

How not to impress the banker

Not only will outright lies leave a sour taste with the banker but if there's an unreported history of bad credit, slow paying habits, accounts for collection, judgments and a bankruptcy, the chances of getting a loan through a traditional loaning institution are to say the least, slim. Here's why.

There are a lot of scoundrels and thieves out there who are out to get anyone and everyone they can. Some of these people buy on credit and have no intention whatsoever of paying their obligation. The sad part of this scenario is that they have such a powerful impact and influence on the credit world—and the credit buying of each and everyone of us.

Credit is built on trust

Credit and trust work hand in hand. The thieves and scoundrels of our society can't be trusted. They are the ones who make most bankers and credit managers skeptical and cynical. Consequently they become extremely cautious and selective in granting and approving loans.

There's not much any of us can do about the thieves and scoundrels because there seems to be an ongoing moral decay regarding debts, debt obligations, and outright thievery. Cheating and stealing (government politicians notwithstanding) have almost become a way of life. Some call it the Age of Greed.

Sadly this phenomenon seems to be growing. Most of those involved in the business, financial, and credit industry believe that it is going to get worse before it gets better. Bankruptcies, collections, bad debts, and bad check writing are running rampant in our society and there is virtually no way to stop it. And that's to say nothing about the $650 toilet seats, $150 hammers, and $300,000 HUD consulting fees. And we've hardly even mentioned the savings and loan scandal.

And do you know who is going to pay for this? You and me. We will pay because interest rates will go higher, prices of products and services will increase, and taxes will climb to cover the costs of the thieves and scoundrels. In the end we all lose.

You've been turned down by the banker: what's next?

A prominent bank officer told me this: "If anyone applying for a bank loan is 100 percent honest, rarely will they ever be turned down for a loan." That says quite a bit—and speaks well for honesty. It means the bankers don't look at all of us as thieves and scoundrels.

This banker also said, "In almost every case where the bank has declined a loan application it's because that person didn't tell us the complete story. We had to find the truth some other place."

The point is that banks do turn people down for credit and loans, but mostly because the individual wasn't honest or didn't give complete information.

There are other reasons for decline such as:

- Incomplete credit application
- Insufficient credit references
- Unverifiable credit references
- Temporary or irregular employment
- Unverifiable employment
- Length of employment
- Insufficient income
- Unverifiable income
- Excessive obligations
- Inadequate collateral
- Too short a period at residence
- Temporary residence
- Unverifiable residence
- No credit file
- Insufficient credit file
- Delinquent credit obligations
- Garnishments, repossessions, or suits
- Foreclosure
- Bankruptcy

Almost every banker will tell you that it is the "hidden factor" not reported at the time of the application that causes most loans to be declined.

The bank cannot refuse credit on the basis of race, color, religion, national origin, sex, marital status, age, or because all or part of income is derived from public assistance. That is the law.

Also, under the Federal Equal Credit Opportunity Act the bank must, in writing, notify you of the reason for denial of the loan. That, too, is the law.

What to do after the decline

The first step to take after being declined for a loan is to find out the reason. This will determine the next steps.

If it's a case that you do not have character, credit, or capacity—which is mostly covered by the above list—probably the next step is to find a co-signer. You will have to find someone who does have the character, credit, or capacity. That means of course, if that person co-signs and you don't make the payments, the bank can go to the co-signer for those payments. That individual becomes totally responsible for your debt.

If you find a co-signer, the bank will notify that person of their responsibility in this manner:

> "You are being asked to guarantee this debt. Think carefully before you do. If the borrower does not pay the debt, you will have to. Be sure you can afford to pay if you have to, and that you want to accept this responsibility.
>
> You may have to pay up to the full amount of the debt if the borrower does not pay. You may also have to pay late fees or collection costs, which increases this amount.
>
> The bank can collect this debt from you without first trying to collect from the borrower. The bank can use the same collection methods against you that can be used against the borrower, such as suing you, garnishing your wages, etc. If this debt is ever in default, that fact may become a part of your credit record."

If this doesn't work, the next step is to seek a loan through a small loan company. They are more lenient in their requirements. Remember though, this means interest will be considerably higher.

If the loan is for a car it's possible that the car company itself may do the financing, such as Ford Motor Credit Corporation, Chrysler Credit Corporation, and General Motors Acceptance Corporation.

If all else fails then the next step is to get spending under control. Now this may not get the loan you need, and isn't the answer you are looking for at the time, but in the long run this is the best solution to any financial problem. In other words, put off buying unless it's an emergency.

The rest is up to you.

5

What to do if You're Turned Down for Credit

"I APPLIED FOR A CREDIT CARD AND GOT TURNED DOWN. I DON'T KNOW WHAT to do." If you've received a letter like one of the following, you are probably wondering what happened and what can be done.

Dear Applicant:

We are sorry we cannot comply with your request for a credit card.

During our investigation, we were unable to verify your independent assets or income through our usual sources. Processing cannot be completed without this important information. Please assist us by having a broker, banker, lawyer, or certified public accountant furnish us with this pertinent information in writing on business stationery.

We contacted the ABC Credit Reporting Agency of Anytown, USA. Although their response did not affect our decision, you have a right to know the information in their file. To obtain it, please contact their Consumer Relations Department. Enclosed is a notice of your rights under the Equal Credit Opportunity Act.

I hope this information is useful to you. If you write to us again, please include the reference number noted above and the date of this letter.

Sincerely,

NEW ACCOUNTS DEPARTMENT

Dear Miss Consumer:

Thank you for your recent application for an ABC Department Store credit account. We regret that at this time we are unable to open an account for you for the following reasons:

- Derogatory credit information
- You have too few satisfactorily rated references
- You do not have a checking or savings account

These items relate to your credit records as reported by ABC Credit Bureau.

Credit bureau information was gained from the following Consumer Credit Reporting Agency. Please contact them with any questions:

ABC Credit Bureau
Anytown, USA

Again, thank you for your interest in ABC Department Store. We would be pleased to consider a new application with updated information should the above reasons change.

Sincerely,

Credit Sales Department

Notice: The Federal Equal Credit Opportunity Act prohibits creditors from discriminating against credit applicants on the basis of race, color, religion, national origin, sex, marital status, age (provided that the applicant has the capacity to enter into a binding contract); because all or part of the applicant's income derives from any public assistance program; or because the applicant has in good faith exercised any right under the Consumer Credit Protection Act. The Federal agency that administers compliance with this law concerning this creditor is the Federal Trade Commission, Equal Credit Opportunity, Washington, DC 20580.

Why would I get turned down for credit

It's not uncommon to be turned down for a credit application. It's certainly something that should not be alarming and create any anxiety because there are some simple and easy ways to solve the problem.

First, under the Fair Credit Opportunity Act you have a right to know why you've been turned down. The above letters illustrate and all notices of decline should include the reason.

Secondly, if you've received a letter of denial, that letter must provide the name and address of the credit reporting agency. The next step is to contact the reporting agency. You might have to do this in person because some agencies will not give out the information over the phone. You can certainly understand this. You wouldn't want someone calling in and identifying themselves as you and then have that reporting agency give out your personal report to a stranger.

Sometimes it may be difficult to find the reporting agency. Most of the major credit card companies check through the national computerized reporting agencies (see chapter on credit bureau for address). Check in your yellow pages for your local office and location.

If there is a local credit bureau there's a chance they will not have the information but they can provide the name and address of the reporting agency if you request. However, they are under no obligation to do so.

When in your local credit reporting agency, ask to see your file even though they are not the agency that did the report. This may cost $10 or so but you'll be able to find out what's in your file.

Spite is not the reason for denial

I can assure you that the credit reporting agency, the credit card companies, banks, and loaning agencies aren't turning anyone down for anything personal. It's a part of business to check each and every application for the risk factor. For sure, they would like to do business with everyone and make the money on the interest they charge. So don't think you're being turned down because they don't like you.

Incidentally, a credit reporting agency doesn't turn anyone down. All they do is report the facts. The company credit manager, where you've applied for credit, either accepts or rejects your application.

Keep in mind that credit losses are astronomical in the credit industry. No firm or business can possibly afford to take a chance without checking the credit history of each applicant. You can imagine what would happen if credit cards were handed out like library cards.

The major causes of credit denial

Here's a list of the major causes for credit rejection:

- No credit file
- Insufficient information in the file
- Insufficient income
- Longevity on the job
- Slow paying habits, poor credit history
- Judgments, garnishments or bankruptcy
- Accounts for collection

In addition there are some causes for turn-down which are beyond anyone's control. Let's take a look at some real life stories and find out various reasons for credit denial.

John, age 59 years, a self-employed carpenter applied for a credit card and was denied. He and his wife own a debt-free home, have a substantial savings account, and all their personal property is clear of any mortgage. Most of their financing has been done through a local bank but other than that they've paid cash for most of the things they've purchased.

He and his wife decided to take a vacation during the winter and thought it would be handy to have a credit card. You can imagine his concern when he received a letter back telling him he did not qualify for a card.

This is a very common case of having no credit history recorded at the credit reporting agency. John and his wife had never before applied for credit, had not used credit cards so there was no reason for any agency to have his file.

He came to me and I recommended that he contact the credit reporting agency and have a file set up. By giving the name of his bank this was a good starter and I recommended that he give a lumber yard as a reference or any other place he might have charged on a 30-day basis. I suggested that he next go to the bank and reapply for a credit card and have the banker give his personal recommendation. If it's an urgent matter most banks will call direct to the credit card company and get almost instant approval.

You know there's a generation of people who were brought up in tough times and never believed in using credit. There are also young people just starting out who have never established credit or a credit file. So it's not at all uncommon to receive a letter of decline based on no file with the credit reporting agency.

Charles is a 25-year-old college graduate with a masters degree. He recently moved from his college town to a large city where he started working full-time with an income of $32,000 yearly. Other than college loans (and there has been no repayment of these loans yet) he has had a limited amount of credit in his college town and none in his new community.

Charles applied for a credit card and was turned down because of no file.

I suggested that he go to a credit bureau serving his community and ask that a file be set up. This, I told him, may cost $5 to $15 but is money well spent because he will want to buy furniture, a car, and a new home on credit. As references I suggested that he give the name of his bank in his college town (making sure the record there was good), and any store or business place where he might have charged. A student loan also becomes a part of an individual credit file and can be given as a reference. I recommended too, that he contact a banker and ask them to give a recommendation for approval of a credit card.

The reason there's a charge for setting up a credit file is that someone has to do the work. In a lot of cases you may have to go directly to the credit grantors and ask that they send a copy of your history to the credit reporting agency.

Young people wanting to move into the credit world who have no credit established, can start by contacting a clothing store or department store and ask to charge. Also bank checking and savings accounts constitute credit reference. Once the accounts are established make certain they are paid off as agreed so that you establish a good credit history.

Insufficient information is reason for decline

Most national department stores and banks, all credit card companies, supply information to credit bureaus. However, your file may not contain all ratings because local retailers, credit unions, and some travel and entertainment and gasoline card companies do not report to credit bureaus or credit reporting agencies.

If you have been turned down because of insufficient credit you will have to contact that bureau or reporting agency and establish additional references from companies where you do credit business.

Correcting disputed or erroneous information

What happens if you discover an error on your bill—goods that were defective when you bought them, or an overcharge by the card company? The Fair Credit Billing Act requires anyone who has made an error to correct these errors immediately without any damage to one's credit rating. Here's a list of those items which are defined as a billing error:

- Something you didn't buy
- Something purchased by someone not having authorization to use your charge card or charge account
- A charge that is not properly defined on the billing
- A charge for an amount different than the actual purchase price
- A service or product that you refused to accept on delivery or that was not delivered according to the agreement
- An error in addition
- A previous payment not recorded on the account
- Failure to send the billing to your current address if the company has been duly notified of the address change
- An item for which you required additional clarification

Notify any correction or dispute by writing within 60 days after receiving the bill. A phone call will not work. In the letter specify the details of the error and include your name, address and the account number.

Anyone who has made an error cannot threaten to use this against your credit record nor can they charge interest during the time of the dispute.

What to do if there's a history of poor credit

Negative information, consisting of late payments, repossessions, accounts for collection, judgments, liens, and bankruptcies will in all probability stop most from getting credit. And of course, any negative information in that file cannot be removed or changed. That information will remain in the file for seven years. If you've been told that this information can be changed or removed you've been misinformed.

If you are unable to acquire credit because of a poor file it's possible to get credit by finding a co-signer. This means that person will be totally responsible for paying the obligation if you don't. Also, there are some credit card companies who will give out a card if you are willing to establish security with them. For further information regarding these cards you can write to:

Bankcard Holders of America
460 Spring Park Place, Suite 1000
Herndon, VA 22070

For a fee of three dollars they will send you a list of those card companies that will give a secured credit card.

Other than that it's difficult to establish credit with a poor record. Therefore, pay as agreed and keep a good history.

Some frequently asked questions about being turned down for credit:

Q. If there's incorrect information in my credit file, can I sue the credit reporting agency?

A. Of course anyone can sue anyone at any time for any reason. But you'd better know what you're doing. In answer to the question, if you've made an attempt to get the information corrected and they have not done anything about it, you certainly have a case. On the other hand, if that reporting agency has made every attempt to get the information corrected there's not much that can be done.

I know of an individual who applied for credit at a department store. The department store got a report on a different individual with the same name who had poor credit. He was turned down at the department store. He then contacted the credit manager and the credit reporting agency. The error was corrected, the credit reporting agency went directly to the department store and advised them of the incorrect report. This didn't satisfy the individual, despite the fact that he was approved. He sued and lost. The judge ruled that the credit reporting agency did everything in its power to correct this error and there was no reason to grant any claim.

Most of the time, with regard to incorrect information, it comes down to the fact that it's something that can be corrected simply through mutual communication.

Q. I live in a small community. There is a local credit bureau and I do have a file there with good information in the file—I've checked it out. I applied through my local General Electric dealer to finance a stove and refrigerator. I was declined credit by General Electric and was advised by the manager of the local store that they had no information on me and they could not approve the loan. I called the credit bureau and they advised me that they never had a call from General Electric. What has happened?

A. Your credit file may or may not be in a number of credit reporting agencies (see chapter on credit bureaus). Apparently General Electric went through a computer reporting agency where you have no file and so came up with nothing. General Electric does not take the time to call local reporting agencies so they cease at this point and decline any applicant.

In smaller communities this is one of the things, not having ratings in the national computerized reporting agencies, that makes establishing credit difficult sometimes. There's not much to do other than go back to the local dealer, ask them to re-apply and advise the company that you do have a file in the local reporting bureau.

Q. I applied for a credit card and the local credit bureau turned me down. What can I do?

A. The credit reporting agency does not accept or reject any credit application. That bureau is only a clearing house of information. All they do is report the facts—provide your history and pay record to the card company, bank or wherever you apply. The credit manager of each respective business either accepts or rejects the application.

The credit reporting agency is only keeper of the records. That record, your pay habits are all made by you. Keep it good.

Q. I called the credit bureau after I received a letter declining my credit. They told me they would not give me this information. Can you tell me why?

A. Most credit reporting agencies will not give out this information over the phone. They have no proof that it's you calling and do not want to give the information out to someone who has no right to it. Your best bet is go there in person and get the information.

Q. What happens to my credit file if I quit charging and pay only cash?

A. At the end of seven years your credit file will have diminished. There will be no record, with one exception. If you've filed bankruptcy this will remain for 10 years.

All file information must remain for seven years. It's the law. That's good information and bad. That's why I stress the fact that it pays to pay promptly. Any derogatory information can be there to haunt you when you want to buy a car or a home or just about anything on credit.

There's one other stipulation in the law regarding this seven-year law of elimination. If you:

- Apply for $50,000 or more in credit
- Apply for $50,000 in life insurance
- Apply for a job paying $20,000 a year

then under these circumstances negative information can be used in the report.

Q. I checked my file and found some incorrect information. My name is Joe Doe and there are four other Joe Doe's. Someone else's information is getting into my file. What should I do?

A. You can imagine the billions of transactions taking place in the credit world. Then consider the similarity of names. It's not hard to understand that errors can be made. It's not being done intentionally.

Contact the reporting agency and have them get the information straightened out. You have that right, and it's the law that they must correct any errors or mistakes.

If they don't cooperate you can report them to the Office of Consumer Affairs or the Federal Trade Commission. Or you can sue them.

Credit reporting agencies don't like lawsuits. They don't even like to think about lawsuits. They're time consuming, expensive, and no one ever wins other than the attorneys.

Most reporting agencies will get on these errors almost immediately because of the threat of legal action.

Q. I went to the credit reporting agency and asked to see my file. They want $15.00. Can they charge me for this?

A. If you've been turned down for a credit card or any credit, and have a letter stating so, then the credit reporting agency, which must be named in the letter, cannot charge you.

On the other hand, if you go to a reporting agency that is not listed on this letter, then yes, they do have a right to charge a fee. It's a matter of them having to take the time and work to get your file.

In all probability you know what's in your file. If you're doing credit business you know how you pay. If you're paying promptly as agreed you have a good record. If you've applied for a credit card and received it instantly you know your record is good.

Finally, if you've been turned down for credit and don't know what to do there is a non-profit organization called Consumer Credit Counselling Service with some 280 offices located in 44 states. You can write to them for the location of an office near you:

National Foundation for Consumer Credit
8701 Georgia Avenue Suite 507
Silver Spring, Maryland 20910

6

Secrets of the Credit Reporting Industry

EXPLAINING WHAT A CREDIT BUREAU IS AND HOW IT WORKS IS ABOUT AS interesting as telling someone how to enjoy watching paint dry. It can be boring. However, there are some interesting highlights in the history of the credit and investigative reporting industry that makes the story worth telling.

How the credit bureau functions

Let me start by giving you a generic definition of what a credit bureau is. A credit bureau or credit reporting agency is simply a clearinghouse of the credit pay habits of all people who do business using credit.

There are about 1,300 independent bureaus or clearinghouses throughout the country. Some are individually owned and others are owned by large corporations. Most communities of 15,000 population have a credit bureau. You might be interested to know, state by state, how many credit bureaus there are that serve each state. Here's a list:

Alabama	33
Alaska	8
Arizona	11
Arkansas	32
California	73
Colorado	28
Connecticut	10
Delaware	3
District of Columbia	1

Florida	52
Georgia	55
Hawaii	2
Idaho	17
Illinois	54
Indiana	42
Iowa	37
Kansas	29
Kentucky	22
Louisiana	32
Maine	4
Maryland	8
Massachusetts	12
Michigan	49
Minnesota	44
Mississippi	25
Missouri	29
Montana	21
Nebraska	21
Nevada	8
New Hampshire	3
New Jersey	5
New Mexico	29
New York	40
North Carolina	39
North Dakota	13
Ohio	45
Oklahoma	45
Pennsylvania	48
Rhode Island	2
South Carolina	25
South Dakota	11
Tennessee	49
Texas	118
Utah	9
Vermont	2
Virginia	30
Washington	23
West Virginia	17
Wisconsin	24
Wyoming	15

Canada has 149 credit bureaus and there are 25 international reporting bureaus.

In addition to these independent credit reporting bureaus there are three national reporting agencies:

Trans Union Credit Information
111 West Jackson
Chicago, IL 60604

TRW Credit Information Services
505 City Parkway West #200
Orange, CA 92668-2981

Credit Bureau, Inc.
1375 Peachtree Street NE
Atlanta, GA 30302

The above three nationwide reporting agencies maintain computer files on almost everyone in the country. On the other hand, the local bureaus have files on residents and consumers in their trade area. Almost all of the local bureaus are tied into one or more of the big three nationwide reporting agencies. That means any one of the bureaus can, within seconds, pull a credit file on anyone in the country.

Anyone who has applied for a credit card, financed a car, bought furniture on credit, mortgaged a home, or completed any other credit dealings has an established record and file in one or more of the above named agencies.

Your history and your file is used by that reporting agency to make money. That's the prime reason they're in business. Here's how that money is made. A simple credit report, verbal or written, costs $1.50 to $3.50. A complete credit report, which includes a courthouse check of judgments and bankruptcies, which is required for any home loan, costs about $35.00. There are some variables on these charges. For instance members often pay less than a nonmember for reports. A membership fee in most of the credit reporting agencies costs about $120 per year. Some credit bureaus also have collection services and there are additional charges for these services.

The credit reporting industry tells us they serve a meaningful purpose—and that is to keep the flow of credit working in our free enterprise system. The Associated Credit Bureaus of America says, "If the flow of credit wasn't controlled we'd all pay more to cover the losses of those who don't pay."

How does a credit bureau work?

As a credit clearinghouse the reporting agencies gather information on all people who use credit. This information is stored in either file drawers or a computer. The information is then sold to credit grantors such as banks, finance companies, retail merchants, credit card companies, and any business or profession that extends credit.

That stored information in those files or computer is the record of how each of us pays our debts and obligations. When a banker or merchant gives us the privilege, and that's what credit is—not a right—of buying and paying later, that grantor has a right to receive this file and from this can determine if they will get their money back as promised.

Sources for all this information

If a banker or merchant did not have the ability to call a reporting agency, granting credit could be somewhat difficult. Here's how that would work. Merchant A would have to call Merchants B, C, and D and find out from them how you paid your bill. This, as you can see, would entail a great deal of time and effort on the part of Merchant A. In fact, extending credit under these circumstances—and in the past it was done this way—in this day and age of hustle bustle financing would be nearly impossible.

Rather, the credit reporting store house, the credit reporting agency, compiles all the information from Merchants A, B, C, and D and then sells the information to Merchant A when you apply for credit there.

Not only does the credit reporting agency store the information from stores A, B, C, and D, but the agency is regularly supplied with credit ratings from oil companies, credit card companies, department stores, mortgage companies, banks, and almost every kind of business that does credit. There's virtually no end of available ratings in our credit-free society.

Not only is the information furnished by these credit grantors but a great deal of the information stored in the credit files is supplied by the individual who applies for credit. As an example, the credit application you fill out includes name, spouses name, address, former address, employer, former employer, income, social security number, whether or not you own a home, name of your banker and other credit references. All this information is incorporated into each respective file as the application is processed.

What about negative information?

Other information that's stored in those files and computers consists of accounts for collection—bills that have not been voluntarily paid. This includes both the paid and unpaid collections.

In addition, public records are checked on a regular basis. This is public information and is legally available and can be legally stored in those files. This includes divorce notices, marriages, court judgments, foreclosures, bankruptcies, disposition of law suits, and tax liens.

It is the burden of each credit reporting agency to file only accurate and correct information. However, it is not the burden of the reporting agency to get any of the information in that file if it is not furnished on a voluntary basis. This is entirely up to the individual. The reporting agency only stores that information as stated above. They do not go out and dig up information.

Who owns that information?

The files and information in those files is owned solely by the respective credit reporting agency. You have absolutely no control over this. That agency has a legal right, upheld in court, to own, control, and sell the information.

Once you've made a commitment to do business on a credit basis then you've also accepted the fact that someone is going to keep a record and that others will check that record.

On the other hand, let's say you don't want to have a credit file. There's a simple and easy answer. Don't use or buy on credit. Or, if you're buying on credit, quit. When you do your credit file will dry up.

Privacy of the file and information

I can't help but think that sometimes it would be better if we could return to the good old days when everything seemed to work simply and smoothly. It seems like then there was some resemblance of privacy.

Or, I've asked, "Were they really the good old days?" I know this about the so called good old days—our lifestyle and standard of living was nowhere near what it is today. And that standard of living has increased and been enhanced substantially because we've been able to use our credit and go out and buy the things that have made our life more enjoyable. So, as we've gained something—the privilege of being able to buy and charge—we've had to give something up—our total privacy.

That so-called total privacy is now stored in some 40 federal, state, and local agency data banks. In addition there are another 40 or so private sector data banks that know about us. It's been estimated that the information in these data banks flows from one computer to another an average of five times everyday. That means this privacy, that information about us, is gone.

Even though it is gone there are still some who believe that it can be stopped. I doubt it. What it comes down to is this: As long as each one of us wants to participate in our free enterprise system—as we all do, as long as each of us wants the privilege of using other people's money, as long as we want the good things in life, it's part of the price we pay. For those who think it can be stopped, I advise you not to get too excited and don't spend too much time and money to get it stopped because I have a feeling it's going to get worse before it gets better. It's built into the system and trying to stop it now is virtually impossible, to say the least.

The reporting industry veil of secrecy

If we really take a good look at the good old days there really wasn't as much privacy as we thought. Things really weren't what they appeared to be, especially in the reporting and investigating industry.

Back in the good old days there were not only complete credit files stored but there was a tremendous amount of personal information flowing freely. Back in the good old days that information not only flowed from one agency and company to another, but the information itself was held in these investigative agencies in total secrecy. In fact, in the 40s, 50s, and 60s there were two impenetrable fortresses in our country. One was Fort Knox, the other was the investigative reporting industry.

There were some 3,400 credit reporting bureaus keeping credit and personal records on each and everyone of us. In addition there were a number of private investigative firms. The principal ones were:

- Retail Credit Company
- Hooper Holmes Company
- American Service Bureau

Back in the good old days the information these companies and agencies compiled, stored, and reported often determined our job availability, whether or not we got car and life insurance, and how much premium we had to pay for the insurance. People's credit, financial, employment, and insurance lives were dictated by these companies. They actually predetermined our destiny on the basis of information that flowed from that agency.

Each report would include information such as name, age, marital status, and children. In addition, race, color, and creed was kept on record. The completed report would include Indian, Negro, and Mexican, and if you didn't fit in these categories you were classified as Anglo Saxon.

There was also such personal information as drinking habits, driving records, moral and personal reputations, family problems, and anything and everything the investigator could dig up. In fact, the worse the information the better the report.

The investigators of these companies would go door to door digging out information, facts, fiction, rumors, or any juicy information they could include in those reports. What the neighbors said—and let me tell you, those neighbors liked to talk—went into the file, lock, stock, and barrel.

Usually the investigation was done in such a sneaky manner that those being investigated had no idea there were people out there going from neighbor to neighbor asking questions. Of course a lot of those neighbors rejoiced and some of them thought it was a good way to get even. So, for most investigators it wasn't difficult at all to get a complete story.

If the investigation didn't get enough negative information from the facts they dug up, quite often there'd be enough information from rumors to build a story. What those neighbors who were spreading the word didn't know was that their names were put on each and every report. Supposedly the supervisor of the inspectors could call to verify the information.

Once the report was completed and the information put in the file it was virtually impossible to verify or change. Regardless of what it said or what information was stored, that person had to live with it. No one could see it, correct it, or verify it.

I knew of an individual who was a heavy social drinker. He was by no means a heavy drinker or an alcoholic. He had no driving violations, no trouble with the law, no accidents. Some of his neighbors thought he drank too much—at least too much for their taste. So they reported that he was a heavy boozer. From that time on this person had difficulty getting car and life insurance and had to pay an extraordinarily high premium. And the sad part is that there was no one he could contact, no way to get the information changed and no way whatsoever to overcome this burden. He could do nothing but pay the price.

Inspectors' competency and efficiency were determined by how much derogatory information was obtained in the investigation. The more negative the better the record looked. If they had a high percentage of turn-downs, which meant that the individual was not acceptable for insurance, credit, or a job, that meant they were doing a good job—at least in the eyes of the company supervisor.

Not only did the inspectors dig for as much dirt as they could get but they also acted as judge, jury, and prosecutor. You see, when they typed up their inspection reports, the first question on each report was, "Do you approve the applicant?" The inspector answered with yes or no. If it was a "no," it was stipulated like this:

- No—Drinking Habits
- No—Divorce
- No—Driving Record
- No—Slow Pay Record

etc. The report then went to the insurance company, prospective employer, or credit grantor, and most times the determining factor was the inspector's recommendation.

Times have changed since then. During the evolution of the reporting industry, and there was certainly an evolution as well as a revolution, those files have been totally destroyed. Can you imagine what they would be worth today in the hands of some attorney?

By the late '60s and early, '70s things started to change. Figures 6-1 and 6-2 are representative of the reports used then. Part of that change can be attributed to a "60 Minutes" exposé about the credit reporting industry. This started the revolution and the next step was the passing of the Fair Credit Reporting Act.

The veil of secrecy has disappeared

Most of this secret type of investigative reporting are gone. The laws covered by the Fair Credit Reporting Act state that there shall be no secret files, no mystical or clandestine investigations, and no closed-door policy and exchange of credit and personal information. Today everyone is entitled to see their file and know precisely what information is in it. In addition, everyone has a right to correct any errors or omissions.

If any reporting agency violates any provisions of the Fair Credit Reporting Act—if they do not allow an individual to check their file or correct the errors, the credit reporting agency can be sued, not only for actual damages but for punitive damages and legal costs. Although, there is one stipulation of that law and any claim, and that is you have to prove the violation was intentional. I might add here that the courts in general have ruled in favor of the reporting agencies if there has been no intent or unless that agency completely ignored the requests.

File_____	**INDIVIDUAL REPORT** Date_____	
Name & address given	Corrected name or address	

I. History and Operation		THIS SPACE FOR USE OF CREDIT DEPT.
A. Age	A.	**APPROVED** ☐
B. Marital status	B.	**REJECTED** ☐
C. Number of dependents	C.	☐ Cr. Cd. No..............
D. Racial decent	D.	Credit Limit $..............
E. Present occupation	E.	
F. Name of Employer	F.	**REASONS**
G. How long in present position	G.	FINANCIAL ☐
H. Previous occupation or location	H.	PAY RECORD ☐
II. Financial Responsibility		REPUTATION ☐
A. Rents, boards or owns home	A.	INCOME ☐
B. If owner, approx. value	B.	FUTURE PROSPECTS
C. Amount of mortgage	C.	GOOD ☐ POOR ☐
D. Approx. salary or income	D.	INDEFINITE ☐
E. Leins & Garnishments	E.	NOT SUFFICIENT
F. Any other sources of income	F.	INFORMATION ☐
G. Estimated net worth		
III. Paying Habits		Date
IV. Character and Habits		Credit Man
A. Personal reputation	A.	....
B. Credit reputation	B.	

The correctness of this report cannot be guaranteed, but was gathered through the most reliable sources available.

Fig. 6-1. This is an old 1950's standard credit report form. All the questions on this form were answered by the inspector. The credit manager, after reading the report, accepted or rejected the applicant on the basis of this report. Often times underwriters and credit managers would decline credit on the basis of race, color, creed and personal reputation and habits information which was included in the report.

CONFIDENTIAL

TENANT REPORT

File No.

CREDIT REPORTS

Acct. No.

_____OFFICE

Rent of premises at   Amt. $

PERSONAL:

1.	Time known (years) by you and each informant?	1.
2.	Are name and addresses correct as given above?	2.
3.	About what is his age?	3.
4.	What is his racial descent?	4.
5.	How many dependents does he have?	5.
6.	Does he have any young children? If so, give approximate ages.	6.
7.	Does he keep any dogs or other domestic animals on the premises?	7.

EMPLOYMENT:

8.	By whom is he employed?	8.
9.	What position does he hold?	9.
10.	How long has he been in his present connection?	10.
11.	Does he conduct his business from his residence?	11.
12.	Does he work full time steadily?	12.
13.	Are prospects for continued permanent employment good?	13.

INCOME:

14.	About what is his annual earned income from his work or business?	14. $	
15.	About what annual income, if any, has he from other sources (inheritance, contributions, rentals, etc.)?	15. $	
16.	If married, does his wife follow a gainful occupation? (What is her individual annual income?)	16.	Wife's Income $

TENANT RECORD:

17.	How long has he resided at present address?	17.
18.	Does he maintain the premises in good condition?	18.
19.	Do you learn that he has ever been dispossessed or sued for nonpayment of rent?	19.
20.	Any complaints from other tenants reflecting on his desirability as a tenant?	20.
21.	What monthly rent does he pay at present?	21. $
22.	Is his rent paid promptly, when due?	22.

REMARKS: Comment on (1) business connections, stability, financial obligations, size of family, reputation and how regarded in community. (2) Landlord experience and how regarded as tenant.

Fig. 6-2. This is a report form used by a national credit-insurance reporting company. The form dates back to the 1960's and was used by landlords who were interested in the history of their potential tenants. Note some of the questions asked and information furnished in a report back then.

The veil of secrecy within the reporting industry has been lifted so that we know now what's going on. However, there is a certain amount of secrecy in that the files are protected so they're not available to everyone and anyone. After all, there's a considerable amount of confidential information stored in those records. The reporting agencies are not an open library of personal information. In fact, if any unauthorized person secures a credit report under false pretense, or if any employee of a reporting agency knowingly and willfully provides a report to any unauthorized person, that reporting agency can be fined $5,000 and the individual giving out the information can be imprisoned for one year.

But listen, let me take a minute and give you some peace of mind about your credit file. As we've said before, that file is a valuable asset and most reporting agencies recognize this. It's not an open book and the information is given out only to those who have a right to use the information—those places where you've requested credit and given authorization to have your record checked.

Competency in the credit reporting industry?

Most of the people in the credit industry are competent. I suppose each and every one of us expects a competency factor of 100 percent by those people who serve us. However, as we all know, no business or profession operates with 100 percent competency. If this would be the case wouldn't it be a perfect world? There would be no lawsuits, no malpractice claims, and maybe no attorneys—or is that asking too much?

So it is with the credit industry. Their competency factor operates at the same level as the rest of our free enterprise society. Like any other business or profession, the reporting industry has its share of slugs, incompetents, and irresponsible people.

I might add here as a footnote that it seems like those who are the slugs and incompetents are usually the ones who are demanding and expecting the highest competency from others.

There is a glimmer of hope, however, and that is with most businesses and professions there are those who are competent and reliable, those who make things happen, and those who make things work in their proper and orderly fashion. They are dedicated, conscientious people working for the well being of mankind. They are the saviors.

Ethics, integrity, and trust?

Because there are these dedicated people in the credit reporting field the industry itself is an ethical and trustworthy business. Those dedicated people have taken it upon themselves to develop the integrity statement, shown in Fig. 6-3 and this is followed by most of them. Let's take a look.

Faith, hope, and trust?

Despite the past history of secrecy, the pitfalls of the business, and the incompetency of some of the people, the credit system seems to be working. When one observes the financial fortunes that have been made, the standard of living each of us experiences, and considers the billions of dollars in credit card and installment debt, you realize that there is some faith and hope.

You may wonder why our society is willing to take chances of borrowing out billions of dollars in products, money and services. In the most part we take those chances on one another because of trust. Credit is built on trust, the trust that the individual or firm who gives credit will:

- Get paid
- That the borrower is able to pay and
- That nothing happens between the time of the charge or loan and the time of the payment

**POLICY STATEMENT ON
INTEGRITY OF CREDIT
INFORMATION**

Recognizing that the integrity and
effective functioning of the consumer credit system is dependent
upon the furnishing, maintaining
and reporting of factual credit
history information, which is a
responsibility shared by credit
grantors and consumer reporting
agencies alike, our company
reaffirms:

1. That consumer credit history
   information will be reported in
   a factual, precise and objective
   manner.

2. That requests by consumers for
   re-verification of challenged
   information will be processed
   promptly.

3. That upon the request of a
   consumer, we will promptly
   review that consumer's account, disclosing to the
   consumer the factual payment
   record as reported to consumer
   reporting agencies and/or to
   other creditors.

4. That unless error is discovered,
   the consumer will be advised
   that the factual credit history
   information will continue to be
   reported.

*Fig. 6-3. This policy statement is the
foundation of the open policy now
used by credit bureaus throughout
the country. Who knows if they all
live by this policy.*

but along with that trust comes a great deal of responsibility on the part of the
borrower. It's good to buy, it's better to buy and charge, but it's best to buy,
charge, and then repay as agreed. That's the sum total of that trust system.

Here are some frequently asked questions about the credit reporting industry:

Q. I feel that I've lost my privacy. I want to know who really has a right to give out
this information?

A. The Federal Trade Commission ruled in October of 1977 that a credit report is
the property of the credit reporting agency. That ruling reads:

> The individual credit file is owned by each respective credit bureau. It is
> their sole means of income, and therefore, they have a right to release
> that information to those persons who have a permissible purpose for
> obtaining the report. To allow a consumer to freeze his file would erode
> the reliability of the consumer reporting industry upon which creditors
> rely to make sound credit-granting decisions.

There are some who would like to freeze their file because the history is filled
with slow ratings, accounts for collection, judgments, and bankruptcies. That

would give them a new "free" run and start charging all over again. Credit clinics are trying to sell those in distress on this idea but it doesn't work. You might want to see why in the chapter "Gimmicks, Tricks, and Credit Schemes to Get Your Money."

Q. I got a credit card and no one checked me?

A. You may not be aware of it but every time you've applied for credit, whether it's for a credit card, bank loan, or whatever, your credit file has been checked. Because you have good credit in all probability the loan or card has been approved, no questions asked, and the fact that your record was checked goes totally unnoticed by you. Most people don't realize that a credit check is being conducted. Most of this work is done behind the scenes.

Even though you are being checked, unbeknown to you, there's nothing to be concerned about. In fact, you can be congratulated if you're getting approved for credit—it means you have a good record.

Q. Can I trust that snoopers cannot get in my file? Can my neighbors or others who have no business see my file?

A. Information in credit reports is controlled by the Fair Credit Reporting Act. The law reads that information can be given out only for the extension of credit or insurance, an application for employment or the issuance of a special license. It is against the law for anyone to get a credit report under false pretense or for the credit reporting agency to give out the information improperly.

Credit reporting agencies do not furnish what is called personal history like drinking habits, health, or any malicious information. There is no "eavesdropping" or "snoopers" information in the files. It is strictly credit history.

That doesn't mean there isn't any negative information in the file because anytime there's a record of collection, slow pay, judgments or bankruptcy and foreclosure this information becomes part of the file.

Q. Does the credit bureau rate accounts?

A. No, the credit bureau only keeps the records. There is no such thing as a rating. The information is only factual, for instance: The bank reports a loan taken out on a certain date for a certain amount, the amount of the payment and when the payments have been made. If the account is paid as agreed this fact is reported.

The Associated Credit Bureaus of America

The Associated Credit Bureaus, Inc. is a non-profit trade organization with its membership made up of all the members. The association represents credit bureaus and debt collection services. They have a government relations office, better known as a lobbying group, with an office in Washington D.C. and also a headquarters office located in Houston, Texas. Any credit bureau can become a member by paying an annual dues.

The Association itself is not a money-making organization and does not serve as a reporting agency or collection agency.

7

Women and Credit

THERE IS NO DOUBT ABOUT IT, WOMEN HAVE BEEN LEFT OUT OF THE CREDIT world and have had to struggle with credit problems most of their lives. In fact, it wasn't until the 1970s that women were even recognized or considered credit buyers. House mortgages, credit cards and charge accounts, as well as the credit bureau credit file itself were all in the man's name. Most single and divorced women were excluded. The credit industry was strictly a male dominated club.

Changing times have changed the role

The radical change that placed women on an equal par with men took place with the enactment of the Equal Credit Opportunity Act. This is a federal law which states that everyone has the right to apply for credit without fear of discrimination on the basis of sex or marital status. What this means then is that credit can be determined only on the basis of credit history and creditworthiness.

Each and every individual's personal credit is an important part of their lives. Therefore, under the Equal Credit Opportunity Act it is no longer legal for a husband to sign for a woman on a credit application. She becomes an individual entirely on her own. However, there are a couple of factors involved that determine creditworthiness. For instance, there must be the necessary property available to secure the extension of credit. In addition, there must be sufficient income to repay the account.

Under the Equal Credit Opportunity Act, a business firm extending credit cannot ask the sex of an individual on a credit application. There is one exception to this rule and that is a federally financed home loan. The government monitors housing discrimination and checks male vs. female house buying. However, even though they request this information, you can refuse to answer.

It is also illegal for a credit grantor to use Miss, Mrs., or Ms. on a credit application. Nor can loaning institutions ask about birth control practices or whether you plan to have children or not.

It is not necessary to disclose on a credit application whether you receive child support or alimony payments. However, it might be a good idea to report this income because it reveals additional buying power and can enhance one's chances of getting a loan.

If at any time a woman feels that she has not been given fair treatment from any credit reporting agency she can and should file a complaint with the Federal Trade Commission or any other federal agency enforcing the Equal Credit Opportunity Act.

Establishing an individual file

Women can request that a credit file be established in her own name at any credit reporting agency. Most of the time, and especially in the case of a married couple, the reporting agency will have only one file and that will be in the husband's name.

It's a good idea for women to have a personal and separate file because in the event of divorce or death she will have credit available immediately. Most women don't bother to set up their own file until it's too late and then get caught in a financial crunch as they are trying to get their lives back in order. Most of the time, those women becoming single under these circumstances are in need of credit almost immediately. If there is no file there is no credit.

Starting a new file is not all that difficult. Go to the credit reporting agency serving your community and request to see the combined file you have with your husband. Then establish your own file by using those ratings which are joint accounts, all assets and property that are in joint ownership—this can include a home loan, credit cards if your name is on them, and any other business account in joint names. Add to that your personal checking account. You must realize that if you pay cash for everything you will not have any credit experience.

There is certainly nothing wrong with women establishing credit accounts because the day may come when you will want to buy a car or a home and you will need a loan to do so. With a credit history this will simplify the application and make loans more readily available.

A new marriage and credit

What happens when an individual gets married? If you take your husband's name the first thing to do is notify your creditors, charge card companies and notify the credit reporting agency. Be sure to use your own first name. Usually what happens in the credit reporting agency is that the records will become one unless you request otherwise.

Divorce and credit

There is no doubt that a divorce can be one of the most devastating experiences there is in life for most women. At the time of divorce a woman not only has to deal with her emotional life but at the same time has to gain control or restructure of her financial life. If she has not already been doing so, she must learn how to make payments, become involved with a day-to-day checkbook, live on a budget, and in all probability lower her lifestyle and manage to live with less income. Sometimes, after a divorce, credit can be the difference between survival and welfare.

During the marriage, credit buying—such as furniture, children's dental work and health care, house mortgage, car mortgage, checking accounts—are all classified as joint accounts. You have a right to use these ratings after a divorce—good or bad. Include in the file any individual accounts you might have such as a ladies' clothing store, or your own dental bill, and be sure this becomes a part of your personal account. Remember though, if there is joint derogatory information that also will be transferred to your personal file. That means that if you and your husband have been slow in paying your house payments or there have been accounts for collection they become a part of your record.

Most of the time the divorce decree will specify who owes what bills at the time of the divorce. However, a creditor is not bound to this divorce decree. For instance, if you have charged at a dress shop and the divorce decree states that your husband must pay this bill, the dress shop does not have to wait until he pays. They can demand payment from you. That divorce decree is between you and your husband and not between you and your creditors. If your husband does not pay the dress shop and it is turned over for collection, that account-for-collection record can become a part of your credit file.

Credit and child support

It is a known fact that very few, and I have heard as low as 20 percent, of divorced husbands pay child support. They simply leave the children deprived of any financial help. That divorced husband usually has no compunction to fulfill his moral or legal obligation. This of course leaves the other single parent, the woman, with the full responsibility of paying the bills. Usually that divorced woman doesn't have the earning power to maintain a household, let alone pay the bills and obligations to support the family.

For a woman with children it's virtually impossible to get by without doing business on a credit basis. On the other hand, it is not the obligation of the credit grantor, the merchant, doctor, or dentist, to support that family. They, too, have to be paid for their services to remain in business. Which then presents a Catch 22—no income, no credit, yet a demand for services, and living expenses—with no child support.

If the child support isn't being paid by the husband, this information can be reported to the credit reporting agency as part of his credit record. Do it! There is a special law covering this which is called the Federal Child Support Enforcement Law. It means the derogatory information, of not paying child support, will become a part of the credit history. It is a debt and obligation owed and will be reported each time that individual applies for credit. Do it! Simply call the credit reporting agency where your former husband lives, refer to the above law, and state the facts to that agency and request the information be put into his file. Do it!

Student and teenage credit

Teen credit has become big business. Sixty percent of all young adults hold part-time or full-time jobs. These jobs represent income, and with the income, teenagers spend. Teenage income represents something like $53,000,000,000 of buying power in our economy each year. Credit-card people, merchants, and bankers know and recognize this market.

Bankers and credit-card companies also know that teenagers as a whole are prompt in paying their obligations, regardless of their assets and income. They seem to take credit seriously.

Some major companies such as Sears, J. C. Penney, and others extend credit quite willingly to teenagers. Their experience has been very favorable and their losses minimal.

What if I do not have a file?

Most young people think they do not have any credit. This is not the case. There are hidden sources of credit—such as a checking account that is maintained satisfactorily. This represents an excellent reference. A savings account can also be used as a credit reference.

Most major credit card companies do not advance cards without some creditworthiness. This means a job with steady income.

Here are three methods by which to establish a credit record:

1. Open a checking or savings account. Make sure the account is maintained satisfactorily at all times. One non-sufficient funds (NSF) check can jeopardize a good credit rating.

2. Apply for credit through a neighborhood clothing or jewelry store. In most cases if the business knows you or your parents they will open an account. Take good care of the account and pay as agreed.

3. Take out a small loan with a bank. Be certain it is a loan with a payment that you can handle. Don't let it get out of hand.

With teen credit comes teen responsibility

Teen credit becomes just as important as any other credit—in fact more so, because with a good teen credit pay record it is much easier to move into the adult credit world. This simply means that if you, as a teenager, take on an obligation, be sure that you fulfill that obligation as agreed.

Sometimes these obligations aren't take seriously. Often this comes from the fact that students haven't been taught the responsibility that goes with borrowing. It is an easy-come and easy-go thing. This has proven to be the case with a considerable amount of student loans.

The delinquency rate with student loans has become a major financial consideration in the country. Students get a part or all of their education and then leave without realizing that they have to pay. Because this has become such a dominate factor in education, the laws are becoming tougher. For instance, the United States Supreme Court recently ruled that a university or college can withhold a grade transcript of a student if he or she is delinquent on their student loan. No pay, no grades.

The United States Department of Education has recently ruled that they will be adding collection charges to past due student loans. That means if that student loan has been turned over to a collection agency, the collection fee can be added on to the balance of the student loan. This can increase that loan by as much as 45 percent of its original amount.

It is only common sense that student loans must be paid the same as any other debt. This becomes a part of the moral fiber of our country. If this weakens and people are able to get by and beat the system, the entire system (you and me) will suffer.

8

Credit Abuse: Who Pays the Bills

ONE-HUNDRED AND SIXTY BILLION DOLLARS REPRESENTS AN ASTRONOMICAL amount of money that it's impossible to comprehend exactly what that kind of figure means. It is so much that we simply lose sight of the significance and after all, "That amount of money doesn't affect me and there's nothing I can do about it anyway?" This seems to be the attitude we take and it is much easier just to ignore what has been happening and eventually it will disappear. But the fact is, the $160 billion dollar rip-off will not disappear and it does affect each and every one of us. Here is how.

The $160⁺ billion rip-off

This $160 billion dollars represents money our neighbors and fellow citizens have not paid and are not going to pay. This means that each and every citizen in this country is going to pay $400⁺ a year to pay their obligations. For a family of four this represents an additional $1,600 a year we pay in added costs for products and services we buy and the taxes we pay—because someone did not pay their fair share.

Time to become alarmed and fight back

If you were told that the government is going to increase your taxes by $400 a year you would get pretty upset and let your legislators know how you feel. There would be plenty of kick-back. Or, if you went through your grocery charge slip and found that they overcharged you $10 every time you went into that store you would dash back to that store in a second and complain about this overcharge. Some of us even shop from block to block to save one to two cents a gallon on gas. Yet, for some reason or another—most likely because of the $160 billion dollars being beyond our comprehension, we just don't seem to get upset or bothered about this $400 a year we pay to carry, like heavy baggage, our fellow citizens who don't pay.

Can we do something about it, other than get angry? Sure we can. There are some steps we can all take to stop this thievery. But first, let's look at the problem:

The Federal Government   The Federal Government charges off to bad debt $32,000,000,000 each year. Some of these debts include loans through HUD, the Federal Housing Administration and Farmers Home Administration. These charge-offs also include student loans that have not been repaid. That is only part of the list. Should these people be made to repay these bills? Where do you think the money comes from to cover the losses?

Internal Revenue Service   The IRS collects one trillion dollars every year. Of this amount they expect a five percent charge-off as uncollectible bad debts. This represents $50,000,000,000 of taxes that people do not pay.

You might ask, "How can this happen?" Here's an example. A small business starts operations, hires employees, withholds income tax from their pay check but fails to send this tax into the government. The business goes broke or is closed by the IRS and there are no assets. The IRS can get a lien which is good for six years, extend it another six years, but have found that after 12 years if the bill isn't paid it becomes "dead." This kind of example goes on every day of the week—many times over.

Credit card industry   Visa, Mastercard, American Express, etc., charge off $13,000,000,000 every year in losses by credit-card holders who do not pay their bills. These are bills that are totally uncollectible.

Bad checks   The Federal Trade Commission reports that there are over $4,000,000,000 of bad checks written in the United States every year—and grows year by year.

Bill collectors   There are 6,000 collection agencies who are members of the American Collectors Association. This association reports that these 6,000 agencies receive $13,000,000,000 of bad debts turned over for collection each year. This $13,000,000,000 includes accounts from doctors, dentists, department stores, and general merchandise stores.

Hospital bills are a major part of these collections. It is reported that if everyone paid their hospital bill, as we are all expected to do, the daily cost of hospital care would decrease by as much as $400 a day. That means when we go to the hospital we pay $400 a day more for services to cover the loss of those who didn't pay.

The American Collectors Association reports that about 35 percent of this $13,000,000,000 can be collected. This leaves $8,550,000,000 which is charge-off to bad debt and becomes a total loss.

Bankruptcy   There are 526,000 individual bankruptcies filed each year in this country, representing $12,000,000,000 of unpaid bills. Then there are 68,000 corporate bankruptcies with a financial loss of $48,800,000,000.

And the $160 billion does not even take into consideration what our wonderful friends in the savings and loan industry have done to us. This is another astronomical amount, not even fully totaled up yet, that you and I are going to get stuck for. Do you wonder why this is called the generation of the greedy?

Who gets stung for these bad debts?

You and I are going to pay, and let there be no doubt about it. Should we become aroused and concerned about these bills we have to pay? You bet. I say we certainly should become concerned and do something about it.

The solution   For some reason or another, our laws have consistently been in favor of the criminal, the offender, the trespasser, and the wrong-doer. The unscrupulous operator usually comes out much better than the victim. Once the deed is done they smile and say, "We beat the system." But do you know something, we are the system and it is us that they beat. And it's time that we get sick and tired of being beaten.

We can do something about this beating and this can be done without costing any money and doesn't take a great deal of time. We should contact our legislators and insist that they crack down on these people who don't pay their bills and taxes and are out to beat the system. To do so, you don't have to start at the top. Contact your local elected government officials. Let them know that it's time that the laws get tougher. Tell them that this is a tremendous loss to you financially.

The only way for us to change this unfair and costly situation—that of all of us having to cover for those who don't pay—is to put the pressure on where it counts. It can be done. Look what happened when MADD (Mothers Against Drunken Drivers) got organized. They complained loud and clear and got new and tougher laws regarding drinking and driving, although there are some who think they aren't tough enough yet. But the point is, if the pressure is put to bear, action will take place.

Restitution   Make them, those who owe and are trying to beat the system, pay. For crimes which do not involve anything other than money, it is senseless to lock these people behind bars and then call it even. If an obligation is due and that person is found guilty of that crime, they should be held accountable for payment in full, plus a sizable amount of interest. This restitution should be a lifetime obligation and not merely for six years, which is the statute of limitations.

Only your law-makers can make the changes—not only for restitution, but a method of follow up—to be sure the job is done. Most agencies involved with restitution are not organized, hence, nothing is being done to make sure these people do pay. Ask anyone involved with child support.

Bad check laws   There is only one way to deal with bad-check writers and that is to enforce strong enough laws that they will no longer want to write these checks. For instance, one state has a law that anyone writing a check for $10 to $500 can be charged $100 to $500 for restitution plus imprisonment of 30 days to one year. Another state law reads for a $50 check the fine is $100 and 30 days in jail, a $50 to $100 check a fine of $1,000 and imprisonment of one year, and a $5,000 check and a 10-year imprisonment. Those laws have meaning if they are duly enforced.

Call for a demand that something be done Don't ask, demand that those agencies involved do something about these abuses and abusers. Those who are abusing the system need to be treated harshly. And if the government isn't capable of doing the job then we should insist that they turn to private agencies to get the job done. If everyone demands that something be done then people will be awakened to the fact that they can no longer bilk the system—the system which is you and me.

And we should demand that each and every person realize that they are part of that system that is being taken. The system is not some abstract being existing outside of ourselves. The system is us.

Our personal responsibility When we think of the $160 billion it becomes so overwhelming that it seems a lost cause and there's nothing we can do. But think of it this way. We don't have to patronize those unscrupulous people who are in business and ripping us off. If the savings and loan industry wants to squander our money, as they have done, there is no law on the book that says we have to continue doing business with them. After all, these people have taken advantage of each and every one of us—why should we support them?

If Leona Helmsley and her kind believe that only the little people, and that covers most of us, should pay taxes, and when these kinds of people milk the system and don't pay their fair share and cheat the government (you and I), why should we patronize their businesses? If we all stayed away from doing business with these abusers and did not support their habit, they would soon get the message that we don't like what they are doing. Then they would stop—this appears to be about the only way there is to stop them.

Those are tough strokes, but they can have an impact on our financial and credit way of life. Unless we all do something, and do it now, there is no doubt it will get worse before it gets better.

In addition to getting tough, we personally can take it upon ourselves to:

- Accept our moral and financial responsibility to one another
- Realize that greed is not alright, especially when it is at the expense of others
- Accept the fact that money and riches can be made honestly
- Pay our just due obligations
- Use our credit cards more discriminately
- Not consider ourselves stupid if we believe in honesty and integrity

Other costs of doing credit business

When we borrow money we pay interest. That's only fair. Loaning institutions are in business for one reason—to make a profit. Their profit is derived from the interest you and I pay.

All lenders, banks, department stores, credit card companies, finance companies, etc., must provide us with information so that we know what interest rate we are paying. This is the Truth in Lending Act law. This information should appear vividly on the loan and explained to you before signing any papers.

We are in a position of shopping for the best bargain when we buy and use credit. As an example, if a car dealer is offering 2.9 percent interest this is obviously better than 10 percent or 12 percent charged by a loaning institution. On the other hand, realize that the car company may only give two years while the bank or loaning agency can give 3, 4, or 5 years. Therefore, the determining factor will not only be the amount of interest, but how much you can afford to pay.

It's also important to know when borrowing how much of that interest is tax-deductible. You may have to consult an accountant to get specific details. But, as an example, interest on a home loan is 100 percent deductible. On the other hand, on a standard or car loan less can be deducted. Thus, at the time you are buying a car it might be good to look into a home-equity loan.

Here are some often-asked questions regarding the cost of doing credit business:

Q. Can one or two percent difference in interest on a loan make that much difference in the total cost?

A. Yes, and before completing a loan, check closely. Here is an example: On a $15,000 loan for three years at 9 percent the payment is $475.86 per month. This means the loan will total $17,130.96 at the end of three years.

That same loan at 11 percent interest has a payment of $489.35 for a total of $17,616.60. That two percent represents $485.64 added interest over 2 years.

Let's take a look at a real estate loan of $60,000. On a 25 year mortgage, 9 percent interest, the payment is $496.78 per month. In 25 years this mortgage costs $149,034.00.

Add the 2 percent to an 11 percent mortgage and the payment is $577.53 for a total of $173,259.00 in 25 years—$24,255.00 additional interest cost.

Q. I bought furniture on credit through a local store. The credit was approved, but now I'm getting a bill and there is an additional charge for interest. Is it legal for them to charge interest?

A. The Federal Truth in Lending Act requires that the creditor (the furniture store) must give you notice of the amount of interest charged and that it be clearly stated. As long as this rate is given, even if the rate is sky-high and far more than rates elsewhere, this interest can be charged. The Federal Truth in Lending Act does not set limits of interest. If you have not been duly notified, all interest charges, past and future, can be removed from the account. Most people are not aware of this and will pay a charge if it's added to the bill.

Q. How much interest do I pay on my credit card?

A. It can vary from state to state, however, in the most part interest on most credit cards is 18 to 21 percent. You sign an agreement to this when you sign your credit card application which covers the terms of the card. Be sure to read them.

Q. What if a company fails to give the required information regarding a loan application?

A. A business is required under the Truth in Lending Act to give correct information, and if they do not abide by these laws, inform the federal enforcement agency, which is the Federal Trade Commission.

You may also bring a lawsuit for actual damages (any money loss) and sue for twice the finance charge. The least a court may award is $100 and the most is $1,000. If you win you may also be entitled to court costs and attorney fees.

9

Choosing the
Right Credit Card

DO YOU KNOW WHY BANKS ARE IN THE CREDIT CARD BUSINESS? FOR ONE REASON and one reason alone. To make money. And money they do make.

If for some reason or another you might have been led to believe that these banks are in this business for any other reason, or if you believe that the credit card industry is a benevolent and magnanimous business that is providing some sort of public service, then you've been hoodwinked.

Credit cards are here to stay

The money that is made, and its potential for profit, has made the credit card industry one of the fastest growing and most profitable financial businesses in our country.

Here's basically how that profit is made. Citicorp, one of the largest credit card companies, or any other bank for that matter, issues credit cards on the basis of being able to "rent" that money at the prime rate. This is usually six to eight percent. Sometimes these large banks can borrow direct from the government on a daily basis, and they do, and the rate can be less than the prime rate.

In turn Citicorp and all credit card banks charge the credit card user anywhere from 18 to 21 percent interest. The cost of managing the credit card processing system, promoting the cards, record keeping and billing costs the banks about three percent. Then there's two percent bad debt write off—those who don't pay their bills. (One reason those of us who use the cards have to pay this high rate of interest is to make up the costs of those who don't pay. This is something we should all be outraged about. Make those people pay, too.) At any rate, this leaves a hefty 5.9% profit. But then that's not all. There's more profit. The card companies charge the merchant, those stores and businesses that use the cards an additional two to three percent.

So, you can easily see why the credit card business is such a highly profitable venture. When one considers that these banks do not have the expenses of inventory, merchandise, or the operation of a factory, and when they can hire and pay minimal wages (and they do) for their help, then it's easy to know why they are in the business. It's also easy to see why they spend almost $54 million advertising and promoting their cards.

When you consider the tens of millions of dollars charged daily on all the credit cards in our credit system, then one can understand why the banks and credit card companies want everyone in the country to have their card.

And frankly, there seems to be some pretty good evidence that they are getting the job done. For instance, do you know that in 1970 only 16 percent of the population held a credit card? Today 71 percent of us—and by our latest census there are 250,000,000 of us—there are some 600,000,000, yes, six-hundred million cards held by one or another of us.

The hustle to get out the cards

There is an overwhelming amount of solicitation on the part of these banks for us to get "their" card. If you don't believe that these companies are over-promoting, look at some of the recent gimmicks.

McDonald's, Burger King, Arby's and Wendy's are all promoting the use of credit cards. Their theory is that if a customer comes into a fast food restaurant with $2.00 cash they will spend the $2.00 or less. However, if they come in with $2.00 cash and a credit card they are apt to spend $7.00 or more by using the card.

Mastercard is now issuing cards to 12-year olds. There's a $100 limit and it's necessary to have the parents consent and guarantee. The card costs $15 and there is an 18.8 percent interest charge. The bank tells us, "This is a way they can build their own credit record." A 12-year old?

To get a bigger share of these high profits some card companies are sending applications to college students who have no credit experience. Other card companies are finding a market with people who are under the guidance of a credit counseling service (these are people who have a history of not paying their bills, the ones we all have to support one way or another) regardless of what their past credit history has been.

What about the future
of the credit card debt

Some economists are questioning the over-zealousness on the part of these companies in promoting these cards. They say, "People are literally being buried alive in debt."

Some economists go on to say that this debt burden is an expense that is going to haunt all of us sooner or later and it is their feeling that this is all being done so the banks can increase their profits. Some even go so far as calling it outright greed.

One of the reasons the credit cards have gotten out of hand is that no one seems to know how to shut it off. Everyone is getting a card—including those who have no financial common sense, those with no fiscal or credit responsibility, and even those who have no intention of paying. There are some who get one card after another because the credit card companies just "keep sending me cards." Their logic is, "They must think I'm a good credit risk because they keep sending cards."

Others live by the theory, "All I need is a Visa, Mastercard, American Express, and Discover card (and it's possible to have as many cards as they'll send) and then all my dreams will come true."

That dream unfortunately turns into a nightmare when all the bills mount up and there's insufficient income to pay. The nightmare usually goes from bad to worse. First, the burden of debts forces them to turn to a credit counseling service, then to an attorney, and eventually into bankruptcy, and total failure. Sometimes we see these people on TV talk shows crying about how they've been abused, not accepting the responsibility on their own.

And the sad part of the entire scenario is that eventually the credit card business comes to haunt all of us. We, the public, pick up the financial pieces by paying higher prices for the merchandise we buy and higher interest on the bank loans. Sometimes it's easy to think they're out to get us.

The credit card conspiracy

As one evaluates and assesses the over-zealousness on the part of the card companies in promoting their cards, it's easy to come to the conclusion that there is an outright conspiracy on the part of these companies. After all, they can't lose. If they have debt charge-offs, they simply increase the rate of interest.

The card companies do in fact go to no ends to get their cards into the hands of anyone and everyone, and then they encourage the card holder to charge to the fullest extent. Run those bills up—that's how they make interest.

Now, I don't personally believe there is a conspiracy or scheme; however, this promotional zest certainly makes it easy for those who have gotten heavily in debt with their cards to blame the card companies for their problems rather than facing the responsibility themselves.

The hook: promoting the card

Most of the banks and card companies are sly old dogs when it comes to promoting their cards. They want to make us think that their card is the only card to have. Here are some of their advertising slogans:

"There Is One Card You Can Always Count On"
"A VISA Card Will Save You Money"
"Make the Better Choice...Choose VISA"
"You Are the One of a Select Few Who Have Been Accepted for a Very Special Privilege...the Prestige and Convenience of the VISA Gold Card"
"Acquiring the Corporate Card Has Never Been Easier"

The card companies also use flattery to make you feel as though you are the only one in the world they are interested in and that they want you to have their card because it's the best. Here are the catchy phrases used in some of their gimmick advertisements:

"With your excellent credit history . . ."
"Because of your company's excellent credit history . . ."
"Not many people are receiving this invitation . . . but then not many people qualify for the VISA Gold Card. In fact, only a handful of individuals, like yourself, have the financial resources and high credit standing required to carry this prestigious card . . ."

One wonders how many millions of these kind of computer printout letters have gone out . . . a handful?

One fact to remember is that card companies can't pre-screen your credit record without your approval.

Secondly, there are many people out there who have extremely poor credit who have received these letters, and some have even received the cards.

The point is that this is all malarky. What's important is to get beyond the glitz and blarney to the raw facts. The main question, and the most important point of getting and using a credit card should be:

How Much Does It Cost?

Choosing the least-expensive card

Now that we know that it's impossible to live without a credit card, the next best step is to find the best card available and one that we can feel comfortable with.

There's a tremendous variety of cards to be had. Each company of course thinks their own is the best. Each card company has a variety of charges and other options. Here are some of the items to check when choosing a card:

Interest Rates: By law, credit card companies must provide notice of the interest rate they charge. It's very important to read the small print on the application and know ahead of time how much interest each particular company charges.

Each bank issuing a card sets their own rate and this can vary from 14 to 22 percent. Thirty-three states have set a limit on what interest the bank can charge. Fifteen states operate with no limit. Credit card companies have set up their billing offices where they can get the highest limit. For instance Citibank, which is headquartered in New York has the billing operation for their credit card business in Sioux Falls, SD. South Dakota is one of the 15 states that operate with no interest limit.

Free Period: This is the time from the date of the invoice to the date the payment is due. Companies vary from 20 to 30 days. Some companies have no free time and interest is charged the minute the invoice reaches the billing office. This can be an important consideration so read the fine point.

Card Charge: Most card companies charge an annual fee from $15 up to $65. Some companies have no charge on the first year.

Each company has different charges. These charges are explained (most of the time in small print) on the application. For this reason it's important to review the application and find one that's the least expensive and offers the best deal.
Here are some samples of the various charges, interest rates, and services provided by card companies.

First Card
FCC National Bank
Box 8870
Wilmington, DE 19885-9435

This company offers its card with no annual fee. However, in reading the fine print we find that there is a hefty 21.4 percent interest charge. There is a 25-day free period which means if the bill is paid within the 25 days there is no interest charged.

VISA-MASTERCARD
National Bank of Commerce
Lincoln, NE 68501

I found an interesting study regarding differences of rates with this credit card. Their application and promotional letter states that the national average for credit cards is 18.6 percent interest. National Bank of Commerce offers 14.88 percent and I verified this by phone. But, the fine print states there is no free period. This means that interest is charged, at the rate of 14.88%, from the time the charge is registered with the card company. Usually this can mean a matter of hours from the time of purchase. So, if the store sends the billing in on the 5th and the invoice isn't sent out until the 25th, this 14.88% interest is charged until the payment is recorded. It's conceivable that there could be 25 to 35 days interest charged.
This same company stated on their application that by replying immediately there is no annual fee for the first year. But there is an annual charge from $12 to

$20 after the first year. I called this bank and asked why the difference between $12 and $20. They stated it depended on what kind of an application has been received, filled in and approved.

At any rate, once the 14.88% interest is analyzed one can find that this could be a fairly expensive card for the first 25 to 30 days.

VISA-MASTERCARD
Norwest of Omaha
Omaha, Nebraska 68102

This bank charges $18 a year for membership, offers a 25-day free period, and charges 19.8 percent interest.

VISA-MASTERCARD
First Wisconsin National Bank
First Star Corporation
Milwaukee, Wisconsin 54303

This bank offers 18 percent interest, $15 card fee, and a 25-day free period.

AMERICAN EXPRESS
World Financial Center, Tower C
New York, NY 10285
1-800-528-4800 or 1-800-327-2177

Once this was considered the status symbol of credit cards. American Express isn't a bad card if you're not looking for extended credit and can pay the bill in 30 days. There is a $55 card charge, plus $30 for any additional card, however there is no interest charged. But, payment is due when the billing is sent. That means if you charge $2,000 this month you pay $2,000 at the end of the month—no monthly payments.

AMERICAN EXPRESS also has a gold card which gives a few additional benefits. The charge for the gold card is $75 a year with an additional card charge of $35. The Gold card has the same terms as the personal card.

DISCOVER
Greenwood Trust Company
Wilmington, DE

This card has no annual fee, charges 18.9% interest with a 25 day free period.

J. C. PENNEY COMPANY

J. C. Penney promotes its own card, having some limitations. Interest charges vary from state to state, anywhere from 18 up to 21%. There is no annual fee for the card.

Beating the system at their own game

This is a good time to point out how to beat the credit card companies—legally and ethically.

Because profit is the motivating force behind the growth of this business these card companies don't like to do business and not make a profit. Here's what I mean.

There are those who pay their invoices within the 25-day free period. This means that the companies don't make any money on these charges. The credit card people and the bank executives don't like this. What it means is that we can use their money for 20 to 30 days for free.

Do you know what they call these people who pay before the banks can charge interest? Dead-beats or 30-day wonders. Listen. If those banks want to do business this way they have to accept this as a part of their business.

Another way to beat the system is this. Card companies charge an annual fee of $15 to $65. When the billing comes for this fee send it back and cancel the card. You'll almost immediately get a letter back stating, as I did:

Dear Mr. Jorgensen:

I am writing in response to your inquiry regarding the annual fee on your VISA account.

Because you are a valued customer I have removed the $20.00 fee for this year. This adjustment will appear on your forthcoming statement.

Sincerely,

CUSTOMER SERVICE REPRESENTATIVE

Little did this person know that I pay within the free period, that I've never paid interest and that I'm considered by their company executives a "dead-beat" or "30-day wonder" rather than a valued customer.

You should also note that some cards have special advantages, such as:

- Rent-a-car insurance
- Travel insurance, Hospital protection
- Medical and legal coverage while traveling
- Lost airline ticket replacement assistance
- Instant cash
- Protection from loss or theft
- Rent a car discounts

If this is all confusing and you're not sure about what kind of a card to order, and you want to know more about the various companies and what they have to offer write to the following firm and they will give a complete run-down of all card companies, which will include interest rates, card charge, and all other features:

Bankcard Holders of America
460 Spring Park Place, Suite 1000
Herndon, VA 22070

Taking out a loan might be cheaper

Charging $1,000 on a credit card means $180.88 in interest. On $1,000 comparable bank loan the interest is $110.25 for the same period.

Tips on protecting credit cards

A most exasperating experience can be that of losing a credit card or having one stolen. It takes time, money, and a considerable amount of adrenalin to get everything straightened out.

The first and most important step is to contact the credit card company immediately. If you take this first step then the credit card company cannot collect for any losses. When making that initial call be sure to keep record of the time, the date and the name of the person you contacted.

Precautionary measures such as the following can often save time and money. To safeguard cards and protect against theft and losses take the following measures:

- Make sure your signature is identifiable as the person authorized to use that card. If you don't, anyone can pick up your card and use it.
- Be certain the card you have has been issued at your request, either as a new card or as a renewal or substitute.
- Keep a record of the cards so that if there is a lost or stolen card you can identify the respective company.
- If your charge slip has a carbon be sure to destroy each carbon after each respective charge.
- Be very careful about giving out your card name and number, especially over the phone.
- Check the monthly statement making sure there are no unauthorized charges.
- Protect that credit card as if it was money itself.

Errors in billing
can turn into a nightmare

It's almost easier to plan a trip to the moon than it is to deal with a computer billing error or an incorrect card charge. Once that error gets into the system there's no stopping it. It's a never-ending process of trying to get it straightened out and off the record.

The error starts at the store where the charge is made. This is the first entry into the computer conspiracy (and everyone will always tell you that it's a computer error). Next, that item is put on the credit card computer. Then the trouble starts. If the account isn't paid on time it appears as an account past due on the company computer. Interest is then added to each billing period and the bills keep building. The next step becomes more hazardous because that account is reported to the credit reporting agency and this then becomes a part of your credit history, and that history means that you are past due on your account. Obviously this can have an effect on any future credit purchases or applications.

And of course, as you know, you can't talk to the computers and they can't talk back. They just keep spitting out this information totally oblivious of the fact that there are extenuating circumstances or any sort of a dispute.

Does this all seem hopeless? Well, it's not. There is an answer, although it's not a simple one. That's why I've said it might be better to plan a trip to the moon.

To get this straightened out it takes some assertive effort on your part. First, contact the store and insist that they get the error corrected. Then have that store contact the credit card company immediately. Next, contact the credit card company and explain very assertively that there is a mistake in this billing and that it must be corrected immediately.

Make certain the credit card company notifies the credit reporting agency. Then you personally contact the credit reporting agency and find out if this rating is in your file. If so, request very assertively that they get it off your record and corrected immediately.

When dealing with a dispute, back up your claim with receipts and all information available. When notifying the store, the credit card company, and the credit reporting agency, be sure to give them your name, account number, and complete details. Get the names of each person with whom you've discussed the problem.

Notify each of the respective parties that you will not (and by law do not have to) pay interest while this account is in dispute. Let them know that this is the law. Also, let each of them know that this information cannot be reported on your credit record until it's cleared up. Let them know that this is also the law.

If the dispute involves a problem with a service or product and you have done everything possible to work out a solution, with no success, then you have a right to withhold that payment from the credit card company, with these stipulations:

- That the charge is $50 or more
- That it occurred in your home state or within 100 miles of your billing address

This, too, is the law.

When everything else fails and there seems to be no solution you can take your claim to conciliation or small claims court. This action usually gets results.

Stores, credit card companies, and credit reporting agenciés don't like to mess with legal problems.

And that takes us to the next stages of the credit world—the legal rights we have and how we are protected by law.

10

Your Legal Rights as a Credit Consumer

BACK IN THE GOOD OLD DAYS THE CREDIT REPORTING AND COLLECTION businesses had their way when it came to rules and regulations. These businesses more or less operated freely and totally without any restrictions and controls. They answered to no one. Back then there were very few complaints filed—in fact there wasn't any place to file a complaint. For the most part these businesses operated by their own decree and even as their own regulatory body.

Because there were no laws and no challenges, the collection business often would use threatening and harassing tactics to collect bills. The credit reporting business held their own tight ship and operated for years in total secrecy.

Because our credit lives are at the mercy of the credit-collection industry, and because these businesses are dealing with the reputations of each and every person in the country, it was apparent that something had to change. Things couldn't continue in such a way and some constraints had to be placed on their activities.

Open season before consumer laws were passed

The first of a series of laws controlling these businesses was passed in 1971, known as the Fair Credit Reporting Act. This law, along with subsequent laws passed, was set up to protect and guarantee consumer rights. The Fair Credit Reporting Act is a document of some 13 pages that covers every phase of the credit reporting industry. We will highlight some of these laws that impact on our credit lives.

New laws give new control over our credit lives

The first impact these laws made on the credit-collection industry was to subject them to legal action if they didn't live by and operate according to the rules and regulations. These legal actions included governmental regulatory bodies as well as civil suits.

Back then few had ever heard of "grievous mental anguish" or "public disgrace and humility." Now of course everyone knows what this means; the people in the credit-collection industry definitely know. And let me tell you, the credit-collection industry detests legal action, not only because they can lose their shirt but because there is tremendous time, energy, effort, and money consumed in litigation. That alone helped reduce the harassment, threats, and secrecy.

In addition to the public having new legal protection with the passage of each law, the consumer was given the upper hand when it came to dealing with their own credit file in the credit world. Each and every one of us was given the right to speak back if at any time we suspected anything going on that was not correct.

To better illustrate how these laws affect our everyday credit lives let's review some frequently asked questions regarding the credit reporting industry:

Q. What information is stored in my credit file?

A. The information stored on each of us in the various credit reporting agencies consists of name, address, marital status, employment, credit history, and public record information. Credit reporting agencies do not include personal information such as lifestyle, habits, and morals in credit files.

Incidentally, let me state that it is specifically spelled out in the Fair Credit Reporting Act that there can be no undue restrictions on the flow of credit information. This means the information in our files cannot be scuttled, replaced, or deleted.

Q. By law, who can obtain my credit report?

A. Your credit report can be used for granting credit, for collecting a past due bill, for employment, and for insurance underwriting. Credit reporting agencies may provide some government agencies with some information.

Q. Can I get a copy of my credit file?

A. Yes. It's necessary to give proper identification, and with this identification anyone can see their own file.

Q. Do I have to pay to see my file?

A. If you've been denied credit there's no charge to see your report. However, if you are just curious to see the file, each reporting agency can charge a fee anywhere from $5 to $15.

Q. Can anything be reported about my race, color, or creed?

A. Absolutely not.

Q. If I apply for a credit card does the bank have to tell me how much interest they charge?

A. Very definitely so, and it has to be clearly explained. In addition to the interest charge they must disclose the cost of the card and the terms of repayment.

Q. What about errors in my file—what can be done about them?

A. The Fair Credit Billing Act states that errors must be corrected.

Q. If I find that the credit reporting agency isn't answering my complaints and they aren't doing anything about correcting the errors, what can I do?

A. The credit reporting agencies are controlled by the Federal Trade Commission. The laws covered by this agency are

- The Equal Credit Opportunity Act
- The Fair Credit Reporting Act
- The Truth in Lending Act
- The Fair Credit Billing Act
- The Fair Debt Collection Practices Act

The headquarters of the Federal Trade Commission is

Federal Trade Commission
6th and Pennsylvania Avenue NW
Washington, DC 20580
202-326-2222

with regional offices as follows:

1718 Peachtree Street NW
Atlanta, Georgia 30367
404-347-4836

10 Causeway Street
Boston, MA 02222-1073
617-565-7240

55 East Monroe Street
Chicago, IL 60603
312-353-4423

118 St. Clair Avenue
Cleveland, OH 44114
216-522-4210

8303 Elmbrook Drive
Dallas, TX 75247
214-767-7050

1405 Curtis Street
Denver, CO 80202
303-844-2271

1100 Wilshire Boulevard
Los Angeles, CA 90024
213-209-7890

26 Federal Plaza
New York, NY 10278

901 Market Street
San Francisco, CA 94103
415-995-5220

915 Second Avenue
Seattle, WA 98174
202-422-4655

If at any time you have trouble resolving any credit, billing, or consumer-collection problem and you don't get a response from the company or agency involved, contact any one of the offices listed above.

Make sure when filing a complaint that you keep record of any and all conversations regarding the dispute. Get the names of the individuals involved in the communication and keep that as part of the record.

The debt collector and the law

In addition to the Fair Credit Reporting Act there is a Fair Debt Collection Practices Act. The purpose of the laws enacted under the Fair Debt Collection Practices Act is simply to make these various agencies treat the consumer more fairly. The "guts" of the act is to prohibit abusive, deceptive, and unfair practices and actions on the part of credit reporting agencies, collection agencies and collectors.

The Federal Trade Commission is quite explicit about harassment, abuses, and unfair treatment. Here's an example of what I mean. Figure 10-1 is an article taken from *The Collector*, a monthly publication of The American Collectors Association.

Under the Fair Debt Collection Practices Act, a law firm in Ohio was found guilty of false threats. This firm said they would sell the debtor's household goods and furniture if the debt wasn't paid. In Ohio, as in most states, households goods are exempt from any forced sale.

A Kentucky collection agency inferred in their conversation with a debtor that they represented the Internal Revenue Service and were trying to collect a debt using this false claim. They, of course, were found guilty of impersonation.

In another Ohio case, The Federal Trade Commission ruled that a collection agency cannot write to an employer to obtain information and state the reason for the inquiry is to collect a debt.

In another collection case a complaint was filed with the Federal Trade Commission that this person received a demand for a $32.00 magazine bill which the

Consent Agreement Carries Harsh Disclosure Requirement

Agency Must Include Notice on Second, Fourth and All Subsequent Communications

By Basil J. Mezines
ACA General Counsel

The Federal Trade Commission recently settled a case against a Texas debt collection agency involving a fine of $155,000 and an agreement to include disclosures in duns to consumers, informing them of their rights under the Fair Debt Collection Practices Act.

The FTC charged that the company illegally harassed consumers with threats of imminent court action, garnishment and incarceration, used obscene and profane language, and threatened them with violence, according to a proposed consent decree filed in U.S. District Court.

The complaint, filed by the Justice Department at the FTC's request, was settled by a consent decree. This means that the case was settled without adjudication of any issues of law or fact and without the collector admitting liability for any of the offenses charged in the complaint.

According to the complaint, the agency's employees harassed, oppressed or abused consumers by:

• Using obscene or profane language.

• Threatening to use violence or other criminal means.

• Repeatedly or continuously telephoning consumers with the intent to annoy, abuse or harass them at inconvenient times and at places distressing to them.

• Falsely representing that the person calling the consumer was a lawyer or a law enforcement official.

• Implying that the consumer had committed a crime and would be arrested or imprisoned.

• Communicating with third parties for purposes other than acquiring information about the consumer's location, without the consumer's prior consent or the expressed permission of a court, and when not reasonably necessary to effectuate a post-judgment remedy.

• Falsely representing the character, amount or legal status of debts that the firm was attempting to collect.

Under terms of the consent decree, which is subject to court approval, the company would pay a $155,000 civil penalty and would be required to make certain disclosures in collection communications to consumers, informing them of their rights under the FDCPA.

Case may set bad precedent

This is probably the most unfortunate development in this case. In the past, collectors have had some success in arguing with the FTC against disclosure provisions and, in at least one case, the court has refused to accept this remedy imposed by the FTC.

This case involves an extremely harsh disclosure provision for a period of five years which mandates that the collector will state in "clear and conspicuous language" in the second written communication, the fourth of such communication, and in all written collection communications thereafter sent to the consumer the following language:

> "Collection agencies must comply with a federal law that grants you certain rights. One of these is the right to have us stop communicating with you about this debt. If you write to [agency name] asking us to stop, we will. But if you owe this debt, you still will owe it and your creditor may continue to collect it from you. This law is administered by the Division of Credit Practices, FTC, Washington, D.C. 20580."

It exceeds previous requests since it must appear in the second, fourth and all communications thereafter sent to the consumer. ACA has been opposed to requirements of this kind because they, in effect, constitute rulemaking which is prohibited by the FDCPA.

The court is asked to impose a mandatory injunction against the collector which parallels the provisions of the FDCPA. Therefore, it should not be necessary to exact the "invitation to complain" to the FTC and the so-called "stop talking provision."

Fig. 10-1. The laws governing the credit industry are very explicit and strongly enforced. This Texas agency was fined $155,000 because they did not comply with the law. It's an interesting case and indicates there are scoundrels out there in the collection business.

person didn't order. The consumer requested that the collection agency terminate collection action. The agency didn't cease collection and sent eight additional letters and threatened the consumer's credit record. The collection agency was made to pay the consumer $10,000 personal injury damages.

Here are some additional questions often asked regarding the laws governing the collection industry.

Q. How, when, and where can a collection agency contact me?

A. A collector or collection agency may contact a debtor by mail, in person, or by phone wherever they can be reached. However, the collector must make this contact during convenient daytime hours specifically spelled out in the law; not before 8 a.m. and after 9 p.m.

Q. Can a collector contact me in person or by phone at my workplace?

A. Yes, unless the collector is notified that the employer disapproves.

Q. Is there any way I can stop a collector from contacting me?

A. Yes. You can contact a collector by mail or phone and ask that they discontinue all communication. However, if you do, the next step most collectors will take is legal action. It's best to communicate and get the problem solved.

Q. Can a collector threaten legal action?

A. Yes, and usually most collectors will proceed, either through conciliation court or small claims court, or through their attorney, with legal action if there isn't an amicable settlement of the account. If a collection agency does threaten legal action they must follow through and not use this threat within itself to force payment. This means, and it is the law, that if they say they are going to take legal action they most likely will.

Q. What can I do if the collection agency breaks the law?

A. The best way to stop illegal action on the part of a collection agency is to report their activities to the Federal Trade Commission or the state Attorney General Office.

You can also sue a collection agency. If you sue and win the case you can recover money for the damages you suffer plus $1,000, plus court and attorney fees. However, if you are not acting in good faith and suing for the sake of suing then you can be held liable for court costs.

Laws that protect the consumer

Following is a brief outline of some of the consumer protection laws.

- A collector cannot use threats or violence to harm your reputation or your property.
- A collector cannot use obscene or profane language.
- A collector cannot repeatedly use the telephone to a point of being a nuisance.
- A collector cannot call you at your work place if you request them not to do so.
- A collector cannot make you pay for collect calls.
- A collector cannot advertise your debt or report that debt to a third party. (However, it can be given out as part of a credit report.)
- A collector cannot misrepresent the amount of the debt. (Sometimes a collection agency will send a bill for $160.00 when the amount is actually $16.00.)

- A collector cannot falsely imply that he or she is an attorney.
- A collector cannot threaten you with being arrested or imprisoned if you do not pay your bill.
- A collector cannot use threats of legal action and garnishment of wages or property unless the collector intends to do so.

The laws and our responsibility

The laws that we have reviewed are only a part of the Fair Credit Reporting Act and the Fair Debt Collection Practices Act. They have been established to protect all of us from undue harassment, abuse, and any illegal methods of collecting bills or reporting our credit.

Those laws protect us but do not give us the right not to pay our just due obligations. In fact, there are garnishment, conciliation, and small claims court laws for the creditor to collect their just due. Actually, the only available law to prevent a debtor from paying his obligations is the bankruptcy law. (See chapter 17 on bankruptcy).

No matter how many laws are passed, the fact remains that credit is a privilege and that any past due obligations of which there is no legal dispute must be paid, or we can expect to suffer the consequences of the law.

New regulations and laws are gaining momentum

The credit industry, which includes credit reporting, collection agencies, credit card companies, banks, and loan companies, in the most part have operated in a relatively unregulated system. Because this is a fast-growing industry, which has a widespread use of credit and personal facts and spending practices of our lives, there are some legislative bodies who are taking a long and hard look at new regulations.

The rules and regulations this industry is subject to are in a constant state of flux and change almost on a daily basis. And like all other governmental tampering some of the laws are good, some are bad.

Whatever the case, there are some new regulations that may be passed within the near future, such as:

- A law that states that if you do not want information concerning your credit card account to be passed on for marketing purposes that card company must cease and cannot disclose the information to others. (This basically applies to those companies who sell their good customer lists to others for promotion of other cards and merchandise.)
- A law that would require a bank, credit card company, or lender to notify you of any unfavorable credit information. (This means if you are slow at the bank they have to notify you before passing on this information.)

- A law requiring a credit reporting agency to report any unfavorable credit information to you each time a report is made.

- A law requiring credit reporting agencies to send copies of their reports to all individuals, at no charge, on an annual basis.

- A law requiring credit reporting agencies to send a copy of their report, at no charge, every time they furnish a credit report to any business or professional firm.

- A law forbidding credit report agencies from reporting delinquent accounts that have been paid in full.

- A law requiring each computer reporting agency to notify every individual that a computer report and data is being collected, and giving each individual a copy of that information along with the source of the information.

- A law restricting banking institutions from disclosing any information concerning the existence or contents of any account, which includes loans, savings, and checking accounts, without the explicit consent of you the customer.

- A law that would require all financial institutions to notify their customers that they have a right to know any information that is passed on and to whom it was passed.

11

Who Gets into Credit Trouble and Why

ABOUT 30 PERCENT OF THE PEOPLE IN OUR AMERICAN CREDIT/BUSINESS/FINAN-
cial society are either slow in paying their bills and obligations or they don't pay
at all. Let's take a look at who they are and the reasons for this neglect.

Who is to blame for the credit problems?

One of the prime causes of credit neglect is what is called financial illiteracy.
Credit neglect isn't necessarily a lack of moral commitment (although there are
certainly some who are morally irresponsible when it comes to financial obligations) but it is more that some people have never been educated on such simple
matters as balancing a checkbook, setting up a budget, making payments, and
managing debts.

Who is to blame? The blame is most likely a combination of many happen-
ings in our lives. For instance, there are some who say financial illiteracy starts at
home. Few parents take the time to teach their children financial and credit
responsibilities. That is certainly part of the credit problem.

Others will tell you that the blame lies with the schools. The question is, "Are
there any preventive finance management courses offered in school?" Of course
the answer is simply that there are none. In fact, students graduate from high
school, and yes, even college, and don't know the first thing about paying bills
and obligations, how to write checks and balance a checkbook, and least of all
have no comprehension of credit card debt. At a major university the question

was asked, "What is debt?" and most of the students answered, "How many payments I'm past due on my credit cards." That certainly isn't what we can call financial literacy.

Educators will tell us that the public isn't interested in financial literacy. It isn't an educational priority. They want reading, writing, and arithmetic. "Teach the students about science, mathematics, and geometry" they say.

And so it goes. No one wants to take on the responsibility and there's not enough pressure from any group to force anyone to do anything about it.

Where then do we get our financial credit management courses? My answer is, "Most of us learn through the school of hard knocks."

Reasons for over-spending

The school of hard knocks started back in the depression era. Those of us who have been through the tough times realize the value of money and are very cognizant of the importance of credit. The fallacy of all this is the fact that those parents who came from the school of hard knocks have all said, without fail, "I don't want my children to have it as tough as I had it. I want them to have a better way of life." That's all well and good and of course these thoughts and feelings have come from the heart and with good intentions. But the problem is, it hasn't taught their children any financial responsibility. In fact, some of these children learned that money, credit, and finances were all easy come, easy go. Dad and Mom wanted them to have a college education, a car, a home, and all the middle class trappings we've heard about as part of the great American Dream.

So what happened? Some of the young generation, coming from this post-depression era, moved into the credit-financial world and assumed that they could get, buy, and charge whatever they wanted. They had not been given any instructions on how money, credit, and financing work. They went out into the business world and soon got into debt over their heads, simply because they didn't know any better. It was a case of having insufficient knowledge and education, along with a lack of parental instruction about the responsibility of handling their finances and living within their means. This cause and effect created a generation of over-spending and over-buying people who have buried themselves deeply in debt. Now they don't know how to get out.

Causes and effects of credit problems

Those post-depression-era children are not the only ones who have built up this uncontrolled mass consumer debt. There are others, who by ignorance, and some by sheer contempt, have added to the debt burden and credit problems of our society. There are also those who have been subjected to extenuating circumstances beyond their control, such as illness, alcoholism, and family abuse. Most of all, there appears to be a strong correlation between credit debt and financial problems, and those who have low self-esteem.

It is a well-known fact that there are some people who depend heavily on financial "things" to fulfill that inner need of acceptance. People with low self-esteem keep buying and buying which leads to heavy debt and credit problems. Assuming this is a correct analogy, let's take a look at the role self-esteem plays in our financial lives.

The meaning of self-esteem

Let me start by telling you that I have no special training or education in psychology, theology, or psychiatry. I speak only from life experiences, insights, some commonsense thinking, and my own homespun philosophy. Therefore you have a right to accept or reject anything I might have to say about the subject.

We can start with some facts. For instance, here's how *Webster's Dictionary* defines self-esteem:

". . . self-esteem: a confidence and satisfaction in oneself. Respect.

Meyer Friedman, M.D., and Diane Ulmer, R.N., MS, in an excellent book entitled *Treating Type A Behavior—And Your Heart*, have this to say about self-esteem:

". . . regardless of the opinions of strangers or friends, if a person's expectations are in excess of his achievements his self-esteem remains inadequate."

They further state:

"If a child is actively disliked or teased by his peers . . . then his self-esteem is bound to deteriorate."

And:

"Having a good self-esteem is knowing oneself, being honest with oneself and having a good feeling about oneself . . . all the time."

That, we can use to a greater or lesser degree to set up our hypothesis for determining the role of self-esteem and our credit lives.

Questioning our own self-worth

Why is it so difficult for us to think and feel good about ourselves? Why is self-esteem so difficult to attain? It certainly seems simple enough. Just a matter of waking up in the morning and saying, "I'm a pretty good person" everyday.

Why is it that we are so tough on ourselves? Why can't we give ourselves credit for who we are and what we are? Why is it so difficult to love ourselves? The answer lies in the fact that we tend to put up defenses when it comes time to look at ourselves. We seem to be afraid of what we might see.

Not only are we afraid of looking at ourselves, but frequently in order to

compensate we will unconsciously pull friends and associates down to that level
we think we are. In fact, Friedman and Ulmer say this about people with low self-
esteem:

> ". . . people who are criticizing other people, often in violent foul lan-
> guage. Anger, impatience, evoke a negative reaction in others . . . inabil-
> ity to achieve lasting friendships."

And they further state,

> ". . . people with low self-esteem are constantly running down other
> people. Ready, willing, and able to spread rumors. Create friction
> between friends and associates. Tearing down people who are more suc-
> cessful than they are."

Causes and effect
of self-esteem deterioration

One can ask, "How can this happen? What would cause a person to reach such a
state that he doesn't like himself and will even take it out on other people, even
his friends?" There is no doubt that there are different reasons for all of us.

One reason for self-esteem deterioration is our environment. Self-doubt and
feelings of guilt are all developed during our growing years. Once these feelings
are developed we then build up defenses and those defenses hide the truth deep
in the unconscious.

In order to find the truth under those defenses there are usually guilt feelings.
These probably have been carried a long time and are embedded so deep in the
unconscious that they are hard to find. Building up those defenses is a way of protecting our feelings of inadequacy. The biggest defense mechanism we build is
that of living a false life and this includes buying material things and getting heavily in debt.

Sadly, the causes of our insecurity, self-doubt, and inability to accept ourselves involve those things that mean the most to us, our family, school, friends,
and religion.

In order to correct our evaluation of ourselves and our self-esteem the best
start is to recognize that something else was involved in developing these insecure
feelings.

Put the blame on school

School plays a powerful role during our developing years. Success and failure is
determined on the basis of grades. And anyone who has experienced bad grades,
or of not living up to our own expectation, knows how this feels. A report card in
itself is a traumatic experience, but to get grades that are poor indicates to a young
growing person that they are dumb. It's hard to erase this strong force.

In school we also have to exist with our peer group. If you're not in with the "in" crowd you are "out." If you are "out," the "in" crowd can belittle one to a point of tears. Kids—students—can be about as mean as any group I've known.

Religion can play a role in developing our self-esteem

Some people might say, "Well here we go again, when everything else fails, blame religion." There is some justification to blaming some religion on the overall development of one's self-esteem. We are told at a young and impressionable age that we are sinners and that we should fear—fear hell, fear eternal damnation, and fear "The Fear of God." And as anyone knows, you can't love something you fear. Love comes from within and one has to love oneself first. Therein lies the fallacy of religion and self-esteem.

A false sense of self-esteem

Sometimes it is easy to think that we can live a false existence. This way we can please others and have more respect. The trouble is, as we live this deception we only dig ourselves in deeper.

Low self-esteem and the shopoholic

Probably the most pronounced illustration of the effects of low self-esteem and credit is that of the shopoholic. Shopoholics are compulsive buyers who buy because they need the "high" they get when shopping and buying.

Shopoholics have a dependency on "things" which they need to enhance their self-worth. They buy clothing and other merchandise and never use them. Often times their closets are filled with items that have never been used and the price tags are still attached.

When a shopoholic goes into a store they get exactly what they need, immediate attention. They are literally waited on hand and foot by every store clerk and merchant in the country. That makes them feel, at least on a temporary basis, important. The merchandise is merely a means to an end, the end being recognition and fulfillment regardless of the price. It is the "high" they need.

The sadness of this is that ultimately the truth comes home to roost—that of paying the bills. The shopoholic is soon confronted with the credit card and other bills which increase their anxiety which can deteriorate their self-esteem and this becomes an emotional and financial sink-hole. And that sink-hole occurs and is fed because people depend so heavily on "things" to prop up their self-image.

Once in this sink-hole it never ends. It becomes a feeling of total helplessness. In fact, as the buying spree and debt burden increases there becomes:

- A sense of failure
- A belief that success is unattainable
- A sense of anger

- A feeling of humiliation
- An idea that the world is against them
- An attitude to blame others for their problems
- A denial that there is a problem
- A fear that someone is going to find out they are in financial trouble
- A lack of control over their lives
- A wait-and-see attitude of what's next and then do nothing about it
- Thought that it is normal to be under financial stress
- A feeling that it is normal to have a collection agency calling all the time
- A belief that there are others out there who are more successful as there is a need to keep up with them by buying newer and bigger "things"
- A feeling that there is no control over life—that's the way things are regardless of what I do

Digging out and rebuilding

It's easy to find blame, easier to complain and do nothing. But that doesn't solve any of the problems. Most of us find it difficult to seek out our own self-realization and self-esteem. We like to take the easy route of not doing so.

I can't cure all the self-esteem problems of life, but there are some simple and easy steps that can be taken, at least to look at what has happened.

First, if you're not sure what opinion you have of yourself, ask this question, "What are the qualities I see in the people I like and respect?" Most likely the answers will be honesty, integrity, intelligence, kindness and consideration, compassion, and concern. Then ask yourself this, "Of these qualities, which apply to me?" You might be amazed to find that some or all apply to yourself. From this you can easily deduct that you are probably a much better person than you thought.

Step two, ask yourself, "Am I a nice person? Am I the kind of person I'd like to have as a friend?" Again you might be surprised with the answer you find. To be a nice person doesn't take that much time or effort. It's mostly a matter of being yourself—unless you're an arrogant mean SOB. If this is the case then there's probably no hope. However, I'm sure you are not an SOB or you wouldn't be reading this book.

The next step is knowing what humility means. False humility will suppress self-esteem. A good way to know your own humility is to ask yourself, "Is it easy for me to accept a compliment?" True humility means doing a good job, succeeding with a task, and then taking pride in the accomplishment. This includes being able to talk about and appreciate compliments from those who sincerely want to congratulate you. Share your successes with family, friends, peers, and fellow employees. People like to hear success stories and tell others. All this will enhance your self-esteem.

A necessary process of rebuilding self-esteem is getting off the financial merry-go-round. We all want to impress our friends and peer group, but at what expense? If you are not rich, then you are not rich and therefore cannot live the life of the wealthy. If you don't have the income to buy expensive things you must plan your life accordingly. The rebuilding of your financial lives starts with living within your means. This may mean tearing up credit cards, wearing older clothing, or buying a used rather than new car. The lesson is that the road to financial recovery is not a road of costly debt ridden "things" to impress other people.

No matter how much you earn, or what position or title you attain, or what possessions you accumulate, you can never depend on those artificial props to attain your self-esteem. You can never be more than what you are. Even with all the blemishes and scars of life you have to face the truth and be yourself. Being yourself means you have to live with what you have, your size, shape, frame and looks. That's it. You can add thousands of dollars of "things" but they won't change that.

Self-esteem, feeling good about yourself, is a powerful force in your life. The feelings and attitude that go along with good self-esteem carry over into every part of your life. Conversely, a lack of good feelings about yourself can lead you into unlimited insecurities with dread results.

Other debt ridden calamities

There are others who get deeply in debt because of various circumstances that are uncontrollable or things that just didn't go the way they should have. This can include divorce, unexpected medical bills, sudden unemployment, lawsuits, or loss of income.

Others get into financial trouble because they just can't handle their finances—income and expenses don't match. Some of these people don't even bother to balance their checkbook.

Then there are chronic over-buyers with incomes of $100,000 a year that get into financial trouble. They just can't handle the financial responsibilities regardless what income. This is self-imposed poverty—big income but no financial sense.

And finally there are those who just plain don't care.

Mercenaries add to credit and debt

Businesses themselves have contributed heavily to an over-burdened debt society. As we've said before, anyone can get a credit card and charge at will. In addition there is a willingness to advance credit regardless of whether the individual can pay or not.

There are loaning agencies, car dealers and realtors who get downright mad if you don't buy—the fact that you can't pay is irrelevant. Making the sale is relevant and means a commission. For instance, there are some realtors who can't wait to close a house sale. Once the sale is completed they get their commission. If the buyer can't pay, the next step is foreclosure, the property goes up for sale again, and this means another commission.

Laying the blame and searching for the causes and effects of credit and debt problems could go on endlessly. However, there is only one person who is responsible.

The weariness of credit problems

No matter what the cause of the credit and financial problems are, there tends to be a time when some people get to the point that they just can't handle it anymore. This often leads to a series of emotional and psychological reactions. Here are some of them:

- Get drunk and temporarily the problem will go away. The fallacy is that drinking takes more money.
- Get back at them...whoever "they" are. "If they are going to act that way I'll show them. I won't pay anything."
- Argue relentlessly about the service, merchandise, or the bill. Tell 'em you've been "taken".
- Write a bad check for the payment. "That'll show 'em."
- Don't show up for work. Call in and say the car won't start and there's no money to get it fixed.
- Feign and blame sickness. This will lead to a real illness which costs more for a doctor.
- Pay one bill rather than looking at the total debt.
- Bandaid the problem with a temporary fix such as a shallow promise to pay.
- Set up a budget and don't live up to it.
- Set up a budget and ignore unexpected bills such as repairs, health services, and holidays.
- Promise payment to the bill collector and don't respond to their calls.
- Fall into a state of depression and hopelessness.

That is the sum total of how people get into trouble, the reasons why, and the reaction to those troubles. Each and every one is avoidable simply by living within your means, keeping your bills paid and not over-extending your income.

12

Over-Extended Credit and Excessive Spending

LIFE'S FINANCIAL STRUGGLE IN ITSELF IS ENOUGH TO DEAL WITH WITHOUT adding the burden of heavy debt. The stress and anxiety of having bills and not having enough income to make the payments is sometimes unbearable and overcoming. In fact, the way I see it, it would probably be easier to walk through a mine field than to dig out of a financial crisis.

There's nothing more devastating than having a bunch of unpaid bills piled up, mortgage payments past due on the house and car, doctor bills mounting, and credit card balances growing by leaps and bounds with interest charges.

Bills, debts, and a lack of money to pay them can make life downright miserable and depressing. That depression deprives us of the ability to do our work as it should be done which leads to more anxiety, less productivity, less income, and an endless sink-hole.

Credit problems are subtle

Credit problems can be, and in most cases are, slow and subtle to surface and be recognized. Most of us don't comprehend what has happened until it's too late. Then suddenly we are faced with debts of disastrous proportions.

Does this have to happen to any of us? Clearly the answer is no. I say no because there are indicators and symptoms that are easily recognized. If they are recognized and corrected it can often save a financial crisis. Let's take a look at 10 of them:

1. If over a period of time there has been a regular savings plan and now there are no longer deposits being made on a regular basis.

2. If, in order to meet living expenses, debt, and house payments, you are using savings to meet these obligations.

3. If each month there is less being paid on credit card bills, leaving a balance and paying credit card high rate of interest.

4. If there is a strain at the beginning of each month to meet debt obligations.

5. When we start charging everyday living expenses that were previously paid with cash.

6. If one credit card is used to pay off another credit card.

7. If there has been at least one consolidation loan to pay off overdue bills.

8. If there's a pattern of paying 30-day bills in 60, 90, or 120 days.

9. If there are collection calls and letters from various creditors.

10. If the charge-card bills are mounting and there are letters requesting that the cards be returned.

The next stages become less subtle and much more stark and harsh. Credit and debt problems begin to control our waking hours and creep into our every phase of existence—extending into the work place, your home, and family life.

The blow that comes next is when creditors start collection action either through a collection agency or through legal methods. This can even mean garnishment or repossession. Obviously these actions affect the work place. Employers don't like to deal with these messy problems of garnishment. You won't like them either. In fact, even the sheriff doesn't like them—nobody likes them.

These activities eventually affect our home life quite severely. Sometimes it can start with an in-house fight over the bills. Who's at fault? How can the bills be paid when there's no money? How come there isn't enough money?

Credit counselors tell us that money and credit problems more often than not are the root cause of marital problems. When the trouble begins, the couples having financial difficulties often argue, pick on one another, blame one another, and become so enraged that there can be physical violence. Those fights may seem to be over domestic issues but most of the time the prime cause goes back to financial strife.

I know of a young couple that got into financial trouble. Both worked, and the wife believed that because she had an income she could spend it just the way she wanted. And what she wanted was to live right now—spend now, and pay later. On the other hand, the husband had a much more conservative attitude and believed in waiting until they could afford the things they wanted. He became concerned about the debt load and wanted to establish a good solid savings account. She, on the other hand, said, "It's my money, I earned it, and I can spend it." At first there were shallow promises by her to quit spending. Ultimately in order to save their marriage and sanity, by mutual agreement, all the money matters were turned over to the husband. Since then things have worked out pretty well and they seem to be back on the road to financial recovery.

Credit problems can be a monster

When we consider all the ramifications of over-buying and over-extending credit, marital strife, turmoil on the job, hardships, and mental anguish, the fact remains that the most common cause of personal-financial crisis, the number one villain that causes more heartaches and more sadness than anything in our financial lives is personal over-spending.

That's an important message. Let me repeat it. The number one cause of financial problems in our society today and the cause of business and personal financial failure is personal over-spending.

Am I coming on too strong? I mean to. That's the gut issue of this chapter. If that message doesn't come across then everything else is irrelevant and unimportant.

Reality or a life of fantasies

How does all this happen? I suppose a part of it is that we all want to live like the rich and famous. We get caught up in our status-symbol society and can't quit. For some reason or another there are those who experience a modicum of financial success, and this could be in a job promotion, an increase in salary, or a business success story, and once the money starts rolling in there's an immediate departure from common-sense spending and financial management. All that new, quick-and-easy money becomes an exhilarating experience, one that a lot of people can't handle. It can be awesome, fantastic, and leads us to believe we can fulfill all our fantasies. It's like a child in a candy store, wanting everything in sight.

The easy money starts flowing and it seems like there's no end to it so there's an urge to spend and buy. First there's a new car, then a new home, a second recreational home comes next, and then other luxuries, exotic vacations, and overseas trips. And of course it's important to keep up with the Jone's—and this costs plenty. There's always another Jone's family just ahead of us and we have to get there.

In some cases, especially in business, there's an attempt to cover the costs of this new standard of living and keep the business going at the same time. Often ends don't meet and it demands more loans and an increase in the debt load. In the meantime there's a struggle because some of the everyday bills are ignored and go unpaid. Pretty soon the reality comes to haunt the business. It's impossible to live on with the expectation of paying for the fantasies and keeping the business afloat—there just isn't enough money to pay for everything.

The "easy fix" to solve financial problems

Often it's impossible to give up a standard of living we've grown accustomed to. Rather than using common sense and rationally solving the overall spending problems, we look for a way out. The illogical thought is, "Get a bank loan." So, it's off to the nearest bank and borrow and borrow. Then the fantasy can be fed and everything goes along well—for a while.

But the borrowing only adds fuel to the fire. This of course increases the debt load and adds more payments. The over-spending in the meantime continues and bank payments come due. Soon there's no money left. Then it's one more trip back to the bank, however, this time the banker foresees trouble and declines any additional loans. This is the beginning of the end which can and will lead to distress, failure, and more often than not, bankruptcy. All this because the fantasy had to be fed and reality was not in focus.

Do you believe this can happen? It's a pathetically true fact of life and happens everyday of the year. In fact, here are a couple of true real-life stories to illustrate how this can develop into such a disastrous situation.

The smaller they are, the harder they fall

When John was 24 years of age he started a small service station business. For all practical purposes he started from scratch. He had very little cash but had maintained a good credit rating simply by buying those things he could afford and paying for them as agreed. Because he did maintain this good credit rating he was able to get financial backing from a major oil company.

I knew John very well. He was gregarious, outgoing, and very personable. He was to say the least a "go getter." He had plenty of ability, tenacity, and something I would call "young guts." He was honest, sincere, and a hard worker. For instance, when a customer came into his station he would sweep out the car, wipe the dust off the dashboard (something very few stations do), check the oil and tires, and give full, complete, and friendly service. People literally lined up to get into his station and it was almost an overnight success.

As time went on John realized he could expand his business and so started a new service, that of cleaning up used cars for auto dealers. This too developed into a dynamic business. For 10 years the combination, his enthusiasm, and a growing business, became a real wealth-builder.

The business grew and more help was hired. The cash flow was tremendous, something John had never experienced before. He was on his way to becoming a highly successful entrepreneur—all but for one thing. He couldn't control his personal spending.

As the money rolled in, both he and his wife bought everything they could get their hands on. First there was a new home, then a new expensive car, next, household furniture—and this included a new baby grand piano. The buying spree went on for about two and a half years.

After two and a half years the buying began taking its toll. There just wasn't enough money to go around. Bills were let slide and then there wasn't enough to meet the payroll. This meant cutting costs of which the first were employees. Business began to suffer because there weren't enough people to do the work. Inventory and supplies were depleted because the bills weren't paid. Everything caved in. Ultimately the business was closed by the bank and creditors and it was the end.

The blow was so powerful and strong that John and the business both just fell apart. John's health deteriorated and eventually he wasn't able to work at all.

That's a tragic story but it's true. The moral of the story and the learning lesson is one to remember: Personal over-spending, extending credit beyond one's means can be devastating.

Personal over-spending and uncontrolled credit leads to disaster

Here's the story of Donald, age 42, an entrepreneur par excellence. Donald, an intelligent, capable, and perpetually optimistic individual invented a unique food product. He started the business (to keep the overhead down) at home. He personally promoted, marketed, and sold the product. With his abilities and enthusiasm the business took off right at the start. It was almost an overnight success story. There was immediate and constant growth and a good profit built in. All in all there were no visible problems and no sign of any weakness.

As the business flourished so did Donald's standard of living, both personal and business. First, the small operation at his home was closed and in place of it a large new plant was built—with an ultra-luxurious office. Then it took money to fill the office building, not only with new furniture but with a national sales manager, a national distribution manager, a CPA, and the secretaries that go along with this operation. Most of the people were given perks and the best of salaries.

At the same time Donald's personal standard of living was upgraded. There was a new plush home—which he could afford. After all, he had a right to cash in on the fruits of his labor. He came from a poor background and worked hard to get where he was. By all means he had a right to expect something in return for his work and effort. But the trouble was there was no stopping. After the new home came expensive trips, vacations, a recreational condominium, boats, and motors, and every other status symbol there was available. Obviously this spending binge put a strain on the cash flow of the business.

Unfortunately at the same time all this buying was going on there was a slippage in his business. Sales became sluggish and this put more strain on the finances. As the sales declined the expenses remained basically the same, so something had to give.

Credit problems take over and push the company over the edge

To make things worse, as the sales declined prices had to be increased to cover the costs of operation. Higher prices meant a loss of some of the market because customers could buy elsewhere for less. Some customers continued buying but became slow in paying their accounts. In fact, the accounts receivable got out of hand. Along with that some of the distributors who were operating on a financial shoestring used the company money to pay their personal expenses. Finally it came to the point where some of these distributors could not pay their bill and had to file bankruptcy. This left the business high and dry.

As the problem multiplied the costs continued. There was no way the business could support all this spending.

Give it did. First the bank foreclosed on the past-due real estate mortgage. The office and plant were closed. Jobs were lost. Cars and trucks were returned to dealers. Bankruptcy was filed and the creditors all took a severe financial loss.

This disastrous situation could have been avoided. In the first place the personal over-spending got out of hand. Secondly it was a case of the business growing too quickly. Management should have taken some time to grow. Thirdly, the owner, Donald, should have waited until it was his turn. The trouble is we all want everything and want it right now. The lesson is, wait until it's your turn. Think long and hard before making any financial commitment, especially if it can't be afforded.

I realize this is hindsight management. Most of us can succeed with hindsight management, but the astute manager will recognize the symptoms before they become problems. That's the only solution.

Look who else got in over their heads

Individuals and small businesses aren't the only ones who have gotten into a major financial mess because of over-spending and poor management. Look at the banks and savings and loan institutions. Most of these companies have grossly over-spent buying pretentious and expensive buildings and offices. In addition they have all hired a multitude of vice presidents who are on the payroll earning $150,000 to $200,000 a year along with grandiose country club expense accounts. Most of these layers and layers of corporate officers have become unproductive bureaucrats who have become an added expensive burden. And that's not the half of it. These same vice presidents earning these big salaries have simply made bad investments that you and I are going to pay for. It's a case of gross over-spending with no common-sense management. And who do they blame? They say, ''It's the economic times, it's certainly not our fault.''

Do you believe their story? I don't. I say they're crying poor mouth and want you and I, the public, to bail them out. If these corporate institutional officers had used some common-sense management they would not have gotten into this dismal financial mess. Are they changing? No.

Alcoholism will not enhance investment skills and improve finances

Fortunes have been lost, small businesses have failed, and individuals have gone broke because of problem drinking. There's no doubt that drinking is one of the major causes of financial-credit failure.

Rarely will a habitual drinker admit to his problem or his financial difficulties. They firmly believe they can make things work and do not see any threat to their business.

The irony is that the alcoholic is usually a fairly intelligent person who could really make things work if they would devote their time, effort, and abilities to business. However, alcoholism is hard to deal with. It's hard to tell an intelligent person that they've got a problem and that if they don't do something it could be the cause of some financial problems.

There is only one solution to solve a drinking problem and that is to quit drinking.

Let me tell you about a young couple who owned and operated a highly successful supper club. The service and accommodations were excellent. The food was outstanding and they really took good care of their customers.

As the business grew the owners kept their bills paid, lived within their means, and really had things going their way—until they started drinking. At first it was just an occasional cocktail, no one noticed. Then it got to be a little more and eventually became a daily habit starting about noon. About this time the service began to deteriorate. Then the drinking became obvious to their customers. Eventually the doors weren't opened on time for business and people just quit showing up. The business and profits declined and eventually the entire operation was closed down. Drinking and driving a business don't mix.

Americans love their cars... debt and all

If there was one single item in our great society that causes more financial problems than any other for the vast majority of us, it has to be the automobile.

The car is the most insidious contraption ever invented to keep us all in constant financial turmoil, in debt up to our neck, and working our tails off to keep up the payments. Cars are monsters that eat our paycheck, our savings account, and keep us from making any sane and sensible investment.

Do you know why I say this? Because the payment on a $16,000 car is about $500 a month. Can you imagine what kind of a savings account one could have at $500 a month, or $250 a month for that matter—$250 for a car and $250 for savings?

Can you imagine what a person making $16,000 a year is doing buying a $16,000 car? It's done.

There's no doubt cars are a necessity. But those expensive luxury cars are by no means a necessity. An essential car is one that can provide good, reliable, safe, and affordable transportation. A nonessential car is one that provides heavy monthly payments, a financial strain and a debt sink-hole.

Over-buying expensive cars is a major part of our over-buying society. It can, for a lot of people, lead to some serious credit and financial problems. They are quite frankly, not worth it.

One final question regarding cars. The next time you go to your auto dealer, ask yourself, "Am I buying this car because I need it or am I buying this car to impress my neighbors and friends?" If you can answer this question to your satisfaction, and you feel you can afford the payment, then you can make a right decision.

13

A Positive, Common-Sense Plan for Financial Recovery

MOST OF THE FINANCIAL AND CREDIT STORIES FROM THE PREVIOUS CHAPTERS have painted a pretty bleak picture. Most people who get into these kinds of situations don't like to face the truth nor do they like to find out who to blame. In fact, the blame can be so elusive that it's easier to just blame others.

Start by finding out who is to blame

There are those who blame the credit card companies, thinking there's a conspiracy and that they (the card companies) "made me do it." Others blame the banks and say, "They should never have let me borrow that money." Some blame the government for whatever reason (and there is some justification for this when we look at the tax bite each of us pays). At any rate, it's hard to pinpoint someone to blame.

There's no doubt that the credit card companies, banks, car dealers, realtors, and department stores promote their services and wares to a point that they become almost irresistible. They make it very easy for us to buy anything and everything whether we can afford it or not. And of course, they want us to charge it because this represents more profit. I wouldn't necessarily call this a conspiracy but it's certainly an enticement most of us can't resist. The weak among us succumb and fall prey to this trap very easily.

Buying and charging is very easy. But when the bill comes it's a whole new story. If there's insufficient income to pay the bills we have to find an excuse or an out. First we find fault and blame someone else. This gives us justification to ignore the bill. Next we receive calls requesting payment. By then we're ready to

111

make up stories like, "I paid cash and my account wasn't credited," or "I didn't get a bill" and the most famous one, "The check is in the mail." The excuses and blame go on endlessly. But those excuses don't work because almost every credit manager has heard them all before. They want their money.

Excuses and blaming others doesn't solve the primary problem—that of solving the financial problem. By using excuses and blaming others we only increase our own anxiety level, which is already plenty high because of the mounting debts with no money to pay them. The time comes when we have to recognize it's our problem, we're to blame, and the buck stops here.

The answer lies in the truth

It's easy to rationalize not paying bills but a time comes when we must face the truth, which is not easy. After all, those "things" we bought and charged are either used up and gone or no longer have that new bright and shiny image they once had. They no longer have the significance they were meant to represent. Now those "things" are only used items and they are not paid for.

The truth comes home to roost

The simple truth is that buying an over-abundance of status symbols does not make life easier nor does it make us look any better, especially if they can't be paid for as agreed.

Respect and recognition do not come from material things. They only represent an extension of a life of lies which ultimately leads to debt, bills, and payments we sometimes can't afford.

You might say about now, "That's easy for you to preach all this, we know the problem, we need a solution."

I don't have all the answers and all the solutions, but there are some that are just plain common sense.

Living a life of fantasies does not solve financial problems

It's only common sense that having the finest and best of everything in life, when we can't afford these things, does not add to our well-being.

Living within our means and keeping our obligations and bills paid as agreed does make sense.

There are some common sense ideas that can save a lot of financial distress and can put a stop to over-spending. For instance, it makes common sense to know how much money we make each month and know how much we have to pay each month for living expenses and to make payments. If we know that the income is less than the expenditures then it's time to stop buying. A simple rule of thumb is to not have payments that exceed 20 percent of our take-home pay— take home pay after rent and mortgage payments have been made, that is.

Take one step at a time in controlling spending

It's not necessary to starve to death or quit living in order to make financial adjustments and get out of trouble. There are some simple steps that can be taken which can cut costs, for instance:

Grocery shopping   Before heading to the store, make a list of items you need. Do this before leaving the house because once you get to the store you'll be faced with a deluge of impulse items. Grocery stores make a fortune on impulse sales. Don't be tempted to buy unnecessary food items. Buy only what you need.

Credit cards   Take an inventory of your credit cards and credit card debt. Eliminate any of the cards you don't need. Cut them up and send them back. Keep one for emergency.

Don't buy because it's easy to charge on the card. This is another case of impulse buying and impulse buying is a credit loser. The only two winners on impulse buying are the merchant and the credit card companies.

Telephone, television, and door-to-door solicitation   Ask yourself, "Am I susceptible to bargain sales, and 'good' deals? Do I have the ability to resist those impulse items?"

Insurance, encyclopedias, get-rich-quick books and sales kits, records, record clubs, book clubs, etc. are all impulse items that do not fulfill any need. Most of these sales gimmicks try to convince us that if we don't buy them we won't succeed or our children will be underprivileged, or we won't get rich like we're supposed to. They make it so easy that all we have to do is call in on a toll-free number, give our name, address, and credit card number and it's ours. It's all so easy—until it's time to pay.

Frivolous purchases   When you see an ad in the paper that shows you how $300 can make you a millionaire, or a promoter will sell you $269 worth of tapes and in 90 days you'll be worth $400,000 in real estate, BEWARE. Save your money; they don't work.

Recreation   We are literally swamped with leisure time activities which include health clubs, boats, motorhomes, campers, guns, cruises, and endless others. They are all easy to buy but hard to pay for.

Clothing   Buy only what you need. Don't buy what you think you need to impress other people. If you're in financial trouble and can't pay your bills, the last thing you need to do is try and impress people with the clothing you wear. Rather than buying new clothing keep your clothes cleaned and pressed. It's a lot cheaper.

Cut costs of everyday expenses   If you're accustomed to going out to lunch, which can be very expensive, quit and carry a brown-bag lunch to work. If you're accustomed to driving to work, which can be very expensive with gas and parking, try taking a bus if one's available, or better yet, walk to work. I know an attorney who lives in Greenwich Village. His office is located downtown Manhattan—a distance of two miles. He walks to and from work everyday. He tells me in the winter when it's cold he can walk to and through several buildings and get warmed up as he goes. The point is, it can be done anywhere.

Expenses vary with the time of the year   Winter to most of us means heavy clothing, fuel for heat and additional car expenses. Plan accordingly. Holidays mean bills, spending, and more bills. Plan accordingly.

Credit is not a magic wand   Credit is so readily available to each and every one of us. We get pre-approved credit card applications every day. There are calls from major department stores that want us to open a charge account. It's so easy that it seems impossible to go wrong. But the realization that once we get the easy credit and start charging there are bills that come with it. Those charges are not magically paid but are paid with hard-earned money—at a high rate of interest. The only magic about that interest is that banks get rich. Don't get caught in the credit card trap.

The spending trap   Life can be going along so well—the bills are all paid, there's a little money left over each month, and there's even a savings account started. There's nothing to worry about. Then we think, "A little bit of buying and charging won't hurt a thing." What starts out to be an innocent plan then turns into a problem. We buy more and more, create a larger debt, think we can afford a vacation, and rather than going coach-class we decide we owe it to ourselves to go first-class. It's hard to stop and we can virtually get caught in a spending trap.

Automobiles   We've talked about cars before. Probably one of the major causes of financial trouble and over-spending is buying a car. The car is the most overrated status symbol there is in our society. Cars will keep us perpetually broke.

What is a budget?

A budget is a self-prepared document which reveals income and expenses and what's left over.

When preparing a budget for yourself, don't lie. You'll only be deceiving yourself and this won't solve any problems.

There are some excellent budget proposals. Figure 13-1 is taken from MONEY GUIDE, published by The Time Inc. Magazine Company, Rockefeller Center, New York, New York.

Preparing a budget

Here is a simple budget form which can serve the purpose of setting up a standard household budget (Fig. 13-2).

Making your budget work

Once you've established a budget, the next step is knowing it will work. If it appears that you have to cut back on some of the payments, contact those creditors who will work with you and ask if they will take less money until you get caught up. Ask for their cooperation and tell them you definitely will pay them.

■ CONTROLLING SPENDING

DO IT YOURSELF

Tracing Your Spending

Fill out this worksheet to start monitoring your income and outgo. Capital gains are your profits from selling investments; mystery cash is money that you spent but can't account for. You can compare your spending in each category with the recommended ranges for three types of households: singles with gross income of $30,000, childless couples with gross incomes of $40,000 to $60,000, and two-children families with gross incomes of $50,000 to $75,000.

ANNUAL INCOME

EARNINGS FROM JOB	$
INVESTMENT INCOME AND CAPITAL GAINS	
GIFTS, INHERITANCES	
ALIMONY, CHILD SUPPORT, OTHER	
TOTAL INCOME	$

ANNUAL EXPENSES

		Suggested spending (% of gross income)		
		Single	Married, no kids	Married with kids
HOUSING, UTILITIES	$	20-23	23-25	22-25
TAXES		17-19	18-20	19-21
SAVINGS, INVESTMENTS		8-9	8-10	8-10
FOOD		8-9	8-9	7-8
DEBT PAYMENTS		8-9	4-5	1-2
VACATIONS, ENTERTAINMENT, HOBBIES		7-9	7-8	5
TRANSPORTATION		7-8	6-7	4-5
INSURANCE		4-5	2-3	3-4
CLOTHING, PERSONAL CARE		4	4-5	5-6
GIFTS, CONTRIBUTIONS		3-4	5-7	5-6
MEDICAL EXPENSES		1-2	2-3	2-3
CHILD CARE, EDUCATION		1-2	1	7-8
UNREIMBURSED BUSINESS EXPENSES		1-2	1-2	1-2
MYSTERY CASH		1	1	1
ALIMONY, CHILD SUPPORT		0-4	0-4	0-4
TOTAL EXPENSES	$			

Source: Shires Financial Group, Littleton, Colo.

Fig. 13-1.   This is a simple but adequate budget which can set a financial record in order.

Your monthly expenses

HOUSING — How much do you spend on housing each month? Include rent or mortgage payments, taxes, insurance and utilities such as electricity, gas and telephone. And figure the average amount you spend on repairs and upkeep each month.

$ _____

FOOD — What are your expenditures at the supermarket and neighborhood grocery store, for eating out and for beverages of all kinds?

$ _____

CLOTHING — What is the average amount spent each month for shoes, dresses, pants, shirts, coats and other articles of clothing? Don't forget those heavy bills when school starts and at other special times of the year. Average them out over the year.

$ _____

TRANSPORTATION — Include your car payments, license and insurance and the amount you spend for gas, oil and repairs each month. Add bus fare and other transportation costs. $ _____

HEALTH CARE — List health insurance payments and bills for physicians, dentists, hospitals and prescriptions. Remember to take an average of what your annual bills would be. $ _____

MISCELLANEOUS — Include all other living expenses such as life insurance premiums, charitable and civic contributions and entertainment. Watch that you don't list items included elsewhere.

$ _____

INSTALMENT PAYMENTS — Add monthly payments not included in the previous categories.

$ _____

TOTAL MONTHLY EXPENSES
$ _____

Your monthly income

TAKE-HOME PAY — Include all salaries that go to support your household. List only take-home pay, not your full salary before payroll deductions. And, do not include overtime pay which can stop at any time. The best thing to do with this is to put it into your savings account. Then, when you have enough to pay cash for something, you can go ahead and spend it, if you wish.

$ _____

VARIABLE INCOME — List any other income you have — bonuses, profit sharing funds, gifts of money, tax refunds, stock dividends and such. What isn't a certainty should be scheduled for savings and then used for special expenses. Funds you know you will receive during the year can be added — and then divided by 12 — to find out what would be available each month. And then be sure you save this amount for your regular living expenses.

$ _____

TOTAL MONTHLY INCOME
$ _____

Fig. 13-2. By simply putting the figures down on paper can be as good a financial problem solver there is. This simple budget can work for any household.

Most will work with you, and there's nothing in the credit world like communication. Communication is the best salve devised to avoid future financial problems. The main point is to live up to the agreement and pay as agreed.

Credit counseling services

If all else fails then it's possible you might need professional help. This help can come from a non-profit organization called Consumer Credit Counseling Services.

Consumer Credit Counseling Services ask such questions as:

1. Are you using savings to pay bills?
2. Are you using credit cards to pay everyday expenses?
3. Are you putting off paying some bills, such as medical, dental, or home, and auto repair bills?
4. Are you taking out loans to pay off bills?
5. Are you extending repayment schedules on loans and bills?
6. Have you reached your credit limit where you can no longer borrow?
7. Are you being contacted by collectors?
8. Are you paying only a minimum due on credit cards?
9. Do you know how much you owe?
10. Are you borrowing from family, fellow employees, and friends to pay bills?
11. Have you borrowed on your life insurance policies?
12. Have you been threatened with legal action?

A "yes" to any of these questions indicates some serious financial problems. If you feel trapped with debt and can find no solution, seek out help from one of these services. Most of the offices provide the service free for the debtor.

According to the National Foundation of Consumer Credit Services there were 180,000 people counseled over the past year, from welfare recipients to doctors.

To find a credit counseling service in your area check your yellow pages under "Credit Reporting Bureaus or Agencies." Or you can write to:

National Foundation for Consumer Credit
8701 Georgia Avenue
Silver Spring, MD 20910
301-589-5600

They will direct you to one of their 300 offices located in almost every state.

How a consumer credit counseling service works

First you must agree to their terms, and their terms are strict. You must agree to set up a budget and to live within that budget. You must agree to stop spending. If you break either of these agreements they will immediately release you from the program and from that point you'll be on your own.

Once you agree to their terms the next step is setting up a payment plan. They will contact all your creditors and ask that they become a part of the plan. Most will agree. Then you must make the payments as agreed. The payments will continue until the service has completed the contract and by then you should be out of debt.

This service is highly recommended. The people involved are serious and know what they're doing. It's certainly a much better way out of a financial crisis than to be hounded by a number of creditors and collection agencies each month.

Each of us of course has the right to do with our money as we please. However, to get the most out of life and get the most use of our money, it's good to plan our spending and have some self control. The rewards of living within our means and keeping our bills paid relieves us of anxieties and worry.

14

Financial Recovery for Small Businesses

WE'VE PRETTY WELL ESTABLISHED THE FACT THAT UNCONTROLLED SPENDING IS one of the major causes of business failure. Over-spending and uncontrolled buying is like walking through a financial mine field.

Getting spending under control

Getting back on the road to recovery isn't all that easy either—but it's certainly possible, if the right steps are taken at the right time. I can add that whatever steps and actions are necessary, they are certainly much better than the alternative—that of going broke or filing bankruptcy.

There's no doubt about it that solving financial problems in a small business takes some major adjustments. First and foremost is getting spending under control. This means a major change in one's lifestyle. It means giving up some of the luxuries of life. But just as important, it means taking a plain common-sense course of action that can and will solve the ailing financial situation. Let's take a look at some of the ways.

Seek help and advice when in financial trouble

First of all, don't carry the anxieties and burden of this heavy debt by yourself. Seek help. If you can't afford professional help ask for assistance from a business associate, a family member, maybe an employee, a banker, but find someone you can talk to and someone you can trust. If you seek professional help—an attorney or an accountant—it can cost money which could add to the debt load. But if that's what it takes, do it.

Look to friends for help

Good friends are hard to come by. But truly good friends can be of help. For one thing, they won't expect that you load yourself with status symbols or that you keep up with the Joneses. At a time when good friends are needed those good friends will stick with you through thick and thin. Those so-called friends you lose because of your troubles, you're better off without. Then at least you won't have to live up to their expectations. You won't lose good friends if you consult with them.

So, choose the right friends and get advice. They can help you get back on the road to recovery and help you ease back into a standard of living you can enjoy. This will provide a lot more respect from them, and anyone else for that matter, than any flamboyant lifestyle you might have built on sand. The respect you will receive from your peer group will be that of a manager with the ability to handle financial affairs successfully.

Seek help from women: the new leaders

I think it's safe to say that women have been laced down for many years and haven't had the opportunity to climb the business and corporate ladders of our financial world. This alone has probably made most women who enter into the business and financial world a lot more persistent and assertive. And let me tell you, there's nothing like having an assertive woman on your side.

A lot of women have taken the bull by the horn and have certainly pushed and shoved, and earned their place in the business-financial world. I say this because in general those women who have become visible and viable in the workplace are, to say the least, very capable and practical.

All this is not to say that women don't get into financial trouble—they do. But in general, I think we can depend on a woman, whether it's a wife, secretary, or business associate, to be considerate, practical, and helpful. They may not be the total answer, but they certainly are worth checking out.

At any rate, regardless of who you seek out—friends, family, banker, women, attorney, or an accountant—get someone to consult with. Don't let false pride keep you from discussing your most intimate business and financial problems. Most people will understand and can be helpful. More important they can provide some much needed emotional support. Just to have someone to talk to alleviates a lot of pressure and some of the anxieties that go along with financial distress.

Going broke is not the way to go

Without help and without consultation there's a good chance of heading down the road of failure. Going broke and failing is final and quite humiliating. Once you're broke you either start all over again or you go to work for someone else. And when you're broke, you're broke.

To avoid failure, recognize the signs of financial trouble. Face the truth, then correct whatever the problem is. Don't wait, don't hide the problem, and don't feel sorry for yourself. Don't above all, look for a scapegoat—it's somebody else's fault. There's only one person in a small business operation that gets into trouble and ultimately gets out—the owner.

Get spending under control, get back on the road to recovery as quickly as possible. Let's see how it can be done.

Start by bean-counting the expenses

I like to refer to the astute manager as a bean counter. Bean counters have the ability to find all the hidden costs and then cut those costs with a butcher knife. Bean counters will go over expenses item by item and see what can be cut and how. For instance, bean counters can go over the following list and see all sorts of holes. Check your operation against these costs—are they under control?

- Insurance
- Postage
- Telephone
- Heat
- Lights
- Utilities
- Payroll
- Taxes
- Social Security
- Rent or Mortgage Payments
- Legal and Accounting Fees
- Capital Investment
- Meetings and Promotions
- Donations
- Car Expense
- Transportation and Travel
- Salaries
- Management Salaries

Look this list over. Are there some costs that are out of line? Are there luxuries and perks eating into the profit? Analyze and scrutinize each and every expenditure, one at a time.

Recovery means making the tough decisions

With a small business, cutting costs of operations are left up to one person. These decisions don't have to be approved by a committee, a board of directors, a department head, or any vice president. They all come down to one person. The decision to cut costs and stop over-spending comes down to you. Once that decision is made, then do it. Don't procrastinate.

Probably one of the toughest decisions any small business person has to make is tightening the purse strings and cutting costs of operation. That's tough because it means upsetting the entire operation, changing plans that everyone has felt comfortable with. And it means possibly releasing an employee or two. Or, it may simply be that of giving up the membership in the country club or any other luxuries that do not produce income. It's a time when tough assertive decisions have to be made—there is no alternative.

When it comes time to make these decisions it's good to have a good clear mind, free of fear and especially free of anxiety. The paradox of course is that over-spending, heavy debt and poor financial management are complete and total anxiety-filled experiences.

The fear of failure can stop growth and recovery of any business

That anxiety eventually leads to fear and fear plays a major role in operating any small business—the fear of failure. There's some justification for this fear. The Department of Commerce recently reported that of all new businesses started, only about one-half survive for two years, one-third survive four years, and one-fifth are operating by the original owner at the end of 10 years.

In order to eliminate the fear of failure it's important to take one step at a time. If there's a fearful event in the business operation, face it immediately. Don't let it fester. Get it out in the open and solve it no matter how difficult it might be. The longer it stays unsolved the more anxiety it creates, and anxiety only creates more fear. An unsolved fear can be an endless trap.

And whatever you do, don't fret and stew about things you can't control. There's no reason to get upset and create anxieties over issues like the 1.65 trillion dollar national debt or the world crises or any other crisis that's out of your control. Don't waste time and energy with these kinds of concerns. They only end up with no solution.

Listen, once you become financially healthy and independent, and when you've solved all your business problems then you might want to take up some of these causes.

Being the cheapest isn't the best and won't solve financial problems

Once the fears and anxieties are under control the next step is to take charge of the inner structure of the business operation. Ask yourself, "If the business isn't making money could it be because the service or product is underpriced?"

There's no pre-determined way to know precisely how to charge for products or services to assure a profit but it's important to know that once the price is set there is a profit built in.

I know an individual who had a small business and showed constant growth. His products sold well. He had good service. But at the end of the year he came to me and said, "I didn't make any money, how come?" I said to him, "Did you charge enough?'' He didn't know. He had never taken time to analyze the cost of the operation. He sold his product at too low a price, had a good income, but the expenses were too great and there was no profit.

Don't compete on the basis of being the lowest priced. Unless you really know what you're doing the chances are you're not going to realize a profit and there's a very good possibility of going broke by being the cheapest. With no profit it's impossible to keep high quality employees and a high quality service. If quality diminishes so will customers.

Know your market

It's not only important to know the price structure of a small business but it's equally important to know the market itself. A small business can fail if management can't foresee the future of its market. It's like the hula hoop—when it's over, it's over. Times change in the market place so quickly.

Have some vision of the future of your business. For instance, if you're in the computer business you'd better be alerted to the fact that this business changes every hour on the hour. When you think you've got a good thing going the next day somebody else is doing it better. And as we all know, computer firms go broke everyday.

I'm sure we'd all like to invent another hula hoop but the possibility of this happening is almost nonexistent for most of us. Those short-lived fads can be troublesome to a small business. It's easy to get in big, buy up a large inventory, and then watch the fad die before it gets off the ground.

Therefore, stay alert to business trends. We have a tendency, some of us small business people, to become moderately successful and then we get fat and lazy with this success. Then one day we go to work and find that our competitor has built a better mousetrap. And let me tell you, there are a lot of mousetrap builders out there in our free-enterprise system.

Negotiate, barter and deal to cut costs

It shouldn't be below your dignity to carry out some cheap-skate transactions within your business operations—and I don't mean stealing. I mean that if you can cut a deal and save money, do it. I've operated my business by being a cheap-skate and it's turned out very well. I'd rather be called a cheap-skate than a failure.

But let me add one thing here. There's one area where you should never be a cheap-skate and that's when dealing with friends, employees, customers, and family. They're too important. Deal as a cheap-skate on material things and possessions.

I've a good friend who operates a very successful business out of a small two-by-four office. The office is adequately furnished but nothing elaborate or conspicuous. People have said, ''Boy, he sure is a cheap-skate—look at that office.'' Most agree it's small and he's cheap, but he's successful. He might have some cheap-skate ideas when it comes to providing offices but when it comes to satisfying his personal and family needs he has the money to do what he wants to do.

To keep costs under control it's a good idea to consider barter. See if you can exchange services or goods. This is a temporary aid but until you get the business back in a healthy financial situation it might work to cut costs.

Learn additional skills to cut labor costs

If you hire marketing and advertising help, consider learning this yourself. Analyze your costs and find ways to do the work yourself. You'll find in most cases that when you pitch in and do some of the grub work your employees will follow right along. They, too, will take it upon themselves to learn some additional skills which can help cut costs.

Cheating will not help solve financial problems

Cheating your customer, taking advantage of a customer, is one sure and quick road to financial disaster. Taking chances on income tax is for fools only. Not paying employees' withholding taxes is a loser. How many businesses have you heard of where the IRS locked the doors because taxes weren't paid? When it comes to IRS and taxes, don't cheat. Take every conceivable deduction you have a right to, but don't deduct something you know isn't right.

Honesty is the best policy. I know that's an old cliche, but it's factual and the truth. Not only do you want to be honest about your product and service, but you've got to be honest with yourself and with your employees.

Greed can lead to financial distress

Greed can be as devastating as dishonesty. Quick bucks, easy money, and get-rich schemes are for the con artists. How often do we hear about some business manager who has been taken by some quick sales gimmick, hot stocks, oil wells, and those "you can't go wrong" deals? Invariably if any business manager gets caught in this trap he's going to lose, and possibly lose everything.

Keeping up with the corporate Joneses is not a method of recovery

It's only common sense that a small business can't provide executive suites, lavish expense accounts, big automobiles, first-class travel, and other perks like that of a large corporation. These things all look good, but for a small business they can often times be a quick trip to failure.

Don't play the game to impress others. Wait until it's time. All these things are much nicer when they're paid for.

Service to humanity costs money

As a small business it's necessary to devote some time, effort, and money to your community. However, know your limitations and set your priorities.

Membership in a Chamber of Commerce is usually a good investment. It's a strong supportive base for your city, community, neighborhood group, and your business.

Support your city, community, neighborhood group, and fellow business people. Buy products when you can from your neighbors. Don't go off to another area or city to buy something you can get right next door. Building a strong neighborhood and community helps build your own personal business.

I can't believe the hundreds of business people I've met over the years who think they can travel many miles to buy a different car or different suit when they can get it within blocks of their own business place. They'll always say, "I got a better deal." That's a pipe-dream which has no foundation. It is excruciatingly painful for a small business manager to see a fellow associate drive around in a new car that wasn't bought in his own community. And this goes for all products, not just a car.

Remember, once that money leaves your community it's gone. When it stays in your community, when you buy in your community the money is kept there to support churches, schools, and the entire operation of that neighborhood or community. It just makes common sense to support your home community. Anyone who can't see this is just plain business-blind.

The national organizations will take your money

There are letter services, organizations, and specialty groups by the thousands. They hound each and every one of us and tell us they can save your business and serve you best. Some tell you they can make you rich.

Some of these organizations will try to convince you that they can lobby for your interests better than anyone else. But first, they need your money. Do you know where that money goes? It goes to pay executives living high on the hog—probably a lot better and higher than you are. Be careful where you spend and send your money.

There are legitimate organizations and all businesses are represented by national associations—The American Medical Association, American Management Association, etc. Join these if you think they represent and lobby for your interests.

When you're trying to cut costs of your business operation, confine your membership to one strong group. Also, confine your activities with these organizations. If you become active and serve on a national board, this might be a great ego trip and usually quite costly, but remember, your competitor is going to be back home while you're spending time and money away from your business.

On the other hand, don't lose sight of good public relations. If there are issues that involve you directly, or those that create a good public image for you, and they aren't too costly, then become involved. If it has something to do with building your business community, get involved. By being involved in noncontroversial issues doesn't detract from good public relations—and it's free advertising.

Your church might be a good example. Spend your money here within reason. However, stay away from controversies like politics. One-half of the people will be on your side, the other half against you. I've seen communities literally tear one another apart over church and political issues. Be careful—don't get involved where you can't do yourself good.

Cut costs by checking your financial contributions

Financial contributions are some expenditures that can contribute to problems you might want to avoid. Excessive political donations, donating for the sake of prestige, will get you nowhere. All politicians are friendly whether you donate to them or not. Don't be led to believe you can buy their friendship.

Excessive church donations won't buy you into heaven. I know of cases where people have tithed themselves into financial difficulties. Give within your means.

Spending time and money with civic and community organizations is all well and good, but don't take valuable money and time away from your business if you can't afford it. I repeat, if you're gone from your workplace, you open the door for your competitor to get your customers.

Don't make waves becoming involved in work that won't do you any good. When you see this happening, it's time to say, "Let George do it."

All this may sound selfish, but why ask for trouble. Be mercenary—you're running a business for the sake of developing a good income so you can take it easy.

Recovery through credit control

A business cannot operate without being paid for its service or products. That's a basic economic fact of life. Businesses go broke if there is no credit-collection control.

If you operate a business that's strictly cash-and-carry, don't change. If you're operating a business that carries accounts receivable, there are only two methods of making certain you don't lose money and go broke. One is to quit charging. The other is to make certain your customers pay their bills on time.

Setting a credit policy

Credit management, like financial management, cannot be operated in a slip-shod manner of guessing and chance taking. That phase of the business has to be well organized just like any other phase of a successful operation. As a credit manager you must be constantly alert and know what you're doing.

The question is, "How do I know when to charge?" The answer is fairly simple. Check the pay record of your customer. In other words, how do they pay their other bills?

Checking the pay record of an individual can be done easily through any reliable credit reporting agency. There are a number of bureaus and reporting agencies throughout the country serving every major and minor market and community. That bureau service is available to any business. It's simply a matter of becoming a member and using the service.

Membership in a credit bureau is not difficult. Call the manager, tell him your needs. They'll explain the service and give you information regarding the Fair Credit Reporting Act. The cost of the credit service is comparatively low—about $10 per month plus the cost of each report.

Listen, if by becoming a member of a credit bureau and using their service you avoid getting caught with one bad risk you will have recovered the cost of your annual dues quickly. Added to that is the fact that if the customer is a good credit risk you have the peace of mind in knowing you will get paid.

Dun and Bradstreet does business reports

Dun and Bradstreet, One Imperial Way, Allentown, PA 18195-0014, does business credit reports. They don't maintain records on individuals but have complete reports on companies and corporations. The services are basically the same as that of a credit bureau but cover primarily services businesses and corporations.

Read and use
the credit report properly to save money

It's important that once you get the information you use it. If a person has a record of not paying bills, that's history and it means he's not going to pay you. Depend on that. Some business managers think they've got a certain charisma and although that customer didn't pay others he's certainly going to pay me. He doesn't want to miss a sale. He knows the customer's a nice person and everyone knows nice people pay their bills. This is a major down-fall of many credit-business managers. They get that negative information and refuse to believe it, thinking, "I don't have to worry, that person is going to pay me." That person won't pay and don't get yourself caught in this trap. Once you've made your decision and turned down that customer don't look back and think, "Did I lose a good customer?" Sometimes a little greed can take over; don't let this happen.

Set your credit policy. If it's 30 days that means 30 days. When the payment is due, it's due and that doesn't mean 31 days or 40 days. Enforce that policy. Don't wait. The longer you wait the more difficult it is to get payment.

Setting a credit policy is not difficult. Let your customer know you appreciate their business but that you've got to be paid in order to stay in business. There's nothing wrong with asking for your money. It can be done in a friendly and business-like manner without upsetting the customer.

Losing control will cost money

So far all this sounds simple. However, despite all the precautions you might have taken to ensure payment, accounts receivable can get out of hand. Here's how that happens. The sale is made. On a friendly basis, built on trust, the charge is transacted. All done on a friendly basis, right? And as we all know, we can trust friends. Wrong. The truth is that the friendship can lead to serious trouble. It can end a friendship, a business association, and can lead to a financial loss.

The first sign of a breakdown, despite all good intentions, is when the friend calls and says, "Can you do me a favor (it's always a favor), I need an extra 30 days to get my bill paid?'' As a friend you don't want to lose this customer and future business so you extend the payment 30 days. At this point you expect that the check with payment in full will be sent as agreed.

However this scenario continues. The payment doesn't come in 30 days. You place a call to your friend who says, ''I'm really sorry about being late but the check is in the mail.'' The check isn't in the mail, it took the phone call to get it and it comes two days later but it's only for 60 percent of what it should be—not payment in full. You're still holding the bag.

The plot thickens. The next phone call is a new pleading, ''Listen,'' says your friend (and about now you're rolling your eyes upward with the thought of the friendship), ''I've got a big sale coming and I'm going to have this money coming in.'' Or another response will be ''I've got this big deal that's going to break if you can just wait.'' Or, ''I'm waiting for a bank loan and I'll send you the money as soon as the loan is completed.'' As a friend, although this friendship is beginning to be over-taxed, you're convinced that he's telling the truth and so you go along with the story.

Now there's more waiting, some partial payments and a request for more merchandise. You've come to the conclusion that if you shut off his business you won't get paid so you take another chance and charge more thinking there will be an ultimate pay-off when you will get the past due balance and payment for the current sale. It's just a matter of time and he'll make it good, you believe.

But no payments show up and somehow or another he's conned one of your employees by saying that you've okayed another charge.

A small payment is made. By now you've learned your lesson so you've shut off his orders and stated that the bill has to be paid before charging any more. But the bill isn't paid. Interest and carrying charges are added and it's now become uncontrollable. In the meantime you learn that he's buying from your competitor—and paying cash.

The friendship by now has ended. Now you have an account for collection, a lost customer, and a bill that's going to be very difficult to collect. You've had to pay interest on the loan to carry this account so you're not only out the money he owes but the interest you have to pay. Next the bill is turned over to a collection agency that will charge from 33 to 50 percent of the bill.

Can this happen? It does happen more frequently than you can imagine. It happens so consistently with small business managers that it can be and is a major cause of business failures.

Don't get caught in this position. Set a credit policy and operate the business accordingly. It's not that difficult. Start by using good common sense.

Eye-balling credit won't save money

There are some business managers who can't turn down a sale because they are so intent on making the sale and the profit that they overlook the important ingredient of getting paid. So they sell everything they can to anyone available. This kind of manager is motivated by profit and they usually have an open door credit policy—kind of like come and get it. Usually those kinds of managers will look at the customer and say, "They sure look good to me." In this way there's no expense of having to buy a credit report and this adds to the profit. The charge is made on the basis of that initial "look" but there is no other control over the credit.

Sound absurd? It's not. There are "eye-baller" credit managers operating in every business and in every community and city throughout the country. A business cannot operate successfully on this basis.

There's one other quirk that gets some small businesses into credit trouble and that's this. Some managers will charge to a customer and then call and get a credit report. This type of credit control doesn't make anymore sense than eye-balling credit management. Collection agencies are filled with accounts like these.

All credit managers have to be totally aware of that person who's going to charge and they have no intention of paying. They are considered free-loaders who are out to get anyone that's vulnerable. They can pick the places and know when they are dealing with eye-balling credit managers. The irony is that these people start out as your friend when they ask to charge. But once the charge is made the friendship ceases. From this point that individual will dispute everything. They will blame you, say the product or service was not acceptable. There are some who say they have paid the bill, despite the fact they know perfectly well it hasn't been paid. Avoid this kind of customer because they can break you. Sometimes these people will even dispute the credit report. In that case just send them to the credit reporting agency and let them deal with it. He won't go there because he knows. What he'll do is go to the next place and find someone who will charge.

If you get to the point that you've got financial problems because of bad debts it's time to take some action. Any account that hasn't been paid in 90 days is a loser. You will have lost profit by this time and probably the possibility of collecting the debt. Just to show you how time can eat up profits look at these statistics:

$1.00 paid immediately is worth $1.00
$1.00 paid in 60 days is worth $.90
$1.00 paid in 6 months is worth $.67
$1.00 paid in one year is worth $.45

Make up your mind that if you have collection problems you have to do something about them. Don't waste your own time on old accounts. Spend your time on new customers or customers who pay their bills. There's no profit in working old accounts. For this hire a specialist. Every credit bureau has a collection department. Use them. Even if you don't recover your money there's a certain amount of satisfaction of knowing that your account will appear on that individual's credit file—for seven years. Everytime someone calls for a credit report that will show up. Before loaning institutions grant real-estate loans they insist on having all collections paid before advancing money.

Credit and collection agencies have about a 40 to 50 percent recovery of accounts for collection. That means all your old bills aren't going to be collected.

That's why it's important that you get bad debts cleared from your records as quickly as possible. There are some collection agencies that won't even list an account if it's over a year old—by that time it's almost uncollectable.

It pays to pay promptly

It's as important for you to pay your bills as it is for your customers to pay you. Credit can make a difference between financial success and failure. Being able to buy on credit means a lot to a small business. If you don't have a record of prompt pay you can lose that right of being able to charge. If you have to pay cash on every delivery it can put a tremendous strain on the business.

That business credit record will be maintained by a credit reporting agency. This means when you need to open a new account with a supplier that firm will check you out. If you have a good record you'll get immediate credit.

If you do have good credit, and the time comes when you need extra time to pay a supplier, that supplier is more likely to grant an extension of 60 to 90 days if he knows he is going to get paid.

Take a positive approach to recovery

How each of us portrays ourselves to our fellow human beings, our customers, and our employees can and will reflect on the business and can determine its success or failure.

When you're down and out, and especially when there are financial problems that seem overwhelming, it's time to take a new look. It's time to add a little pizzazz to the business. It's time to get some new and fresh ideas going.

Start by developing a good feeling about yourself and your business. How we portray ourselves to customers and especially to employees will reflect on the business and can determine its success or failure.

To establish that good feeling, start by becoming obsessed with a positive attitude. Eliminate all negativism. Don't let yourself get into a negative frame of mind. That can and will carry over to your associates. If you treat those people around you, your employees and customers, with a callous attitude, those customers are going to go elsewhere and employees are not going to be enthusiastic about working in your business.

Eliminate fear
from the workplace; this will pay off

Once employees lose their enthusiasm, they become fearful about their job status. We've talked about the fear of failure in a business operation and what effect it can have on its overall success or failure. Now let's look at fear in the workplace.

The fear of making a mistake, the fear of being reprimanded, and the fear of being fired are ever present in a workplace that doesn't show compassion. If an employee makes a mistake, get them corrected and then get on with other things.

The best that can come from a mistake is that it becomes a learning experience. Don't make it anymore than that.

All employees need freedom to exercise their mental abilities and their creativity. If they become filled with fear they won't come forward with new ideas. I'm convinced that if an employee is not encouraged everytime he or she makes a suggestion, pretty soon they will quit thinking and creating. This can be a tremendous loss to a business because almost every business, especially a small business operation, depends on new fresh and innovative ideas to keep ahead of the competition.

To get the most from your fellow workers and employees tell them how much you appreciate what they are doing. Show your appreciation with promotions and financial rewards. Pay employees a fair salary, treat them with dignity, recognize their potential, and give them responsibility. If they do, they will stay with you a long time, and longevity is an important ingredient to the success of a business.

On the other hand, if you create an atmosphere in the workplace where those employees are restless and don't really know where you stand they're going to be constantly looking for a better job.

Don't use employees to the point they they literally wear out and grind down to nothing. They can lose money. It's a very subtle thing that can happen and often isn't noticeable on a day-to-day basis, but it can happen.

Don't treat employees as machines. This may have worked back in the days of the sweat shops but today it's a different world. People are now well educated and very mobile. They no longer have to stay on a job they don't like.

You know, work is an important part of any employee's life. They probably spend 70 to 80 percent of their waking hours at work. They want to take pride in their work and their workplace. They want to call it their business. The fact is, most people like to brag about their job, their boss, and their workplace—if they have something to brag about.

Create such a good positive atmosphere in your organization that when those employees are away from their job they'll praise you and your business. Don't give them any reason to leave their workplace with a chip on their shoulder. If they talk to their friends and peer group about you in a negative manner it doesn't do any business any good.

This is one advantage of having a small business rather than a large corporation, the fact that you can deal with each person on a personal basis. Let the corporation hire the robots.

Personnel problem-solving saves time and money

Internal disputes, personality clashes, envy, and internal sexual activities are all problems that create an unhealthy atmosphere in the workplace. Solve them and eliminate them.

Establish a good communication with employees. Don't let them sit around and talk with one another about something that's upsetting them. Complaining nurtures discontent, discontent nurtures slovenliness which all leads to failure.

Don't let personal disputes take hold in your business. Get them settled and quickly. It's done through an open-door policy. If the door is closed for any employee you're asking for trouble.

On the other hand, don't become personally involved with employees and don't let your emotions become involved.

That job is important to that employee. They want to take pride in it. Give them every reason in the world to brag about their job, because that's the greatest and least expensive advertising you can get.

Measuring job performance to enhance profits

I recently read a book about job performance by a college educator which covers the following:

- Assessing sales performance
- Sales force management and planning
- Manpower planning for the small company
- Setting personnel policies
- Dollars spent on customers
- Etc.

Does that sound like something you can deal with? If you've got a lot of time, money, and manpower you might be able to get something out of this. But most of us don't have that kind of personnel.

It is my belief that complication only creates more problems and costs money. The best way to deal with employees performance is keeping it simple and using common sense. Don't set up quotas, diagrams, system analyses, etc. Let there be a free spirit among your employees and they'll produce and perform.

Hiring new employees to enhance financial security

As you hire any new employee, knowing if that person you hire will earn their way is very important. Not only do you want them to earn their salary and expenses but you've got to make sure they earn a profit for the business. There are people who can sluff off through a job and never produce. They look busy, they're on the go and move about in the workplace giving the impression that they are really producing. Most of these types work so hard trying to look busy that they get tired out because it's more of a grind to look busy than to just get the work done. For some reason or another they don't have the initiative and drive to take that extra step that is so important in building a successful and profitable business.

Look for bright and positive people who will take pride in their work. Think of the negative people you've encountered. Think of how their attitude affected you. Would you want them to work for you? They turn off customers and can hurt a small growing business.

Let motivation create success

Motivating employees can help any business. I know a small company with 20 employees. The owner treats these employees with total disdain. Because of this attitude there's a constant turn-over. This means rehiring and retraining. This type of treatment discourages any motivation on the part of employees.

Service is your most important product and can take a failing business into profit

One of the least expensive and most productive elements of any small business is service.

A small business firm has a tremendous advantage over a giant corporation when it comes to service. Sometimes the large corporation gets lazy and when they do it's time for the small operator to move in. For one thing a small business doesn't have to meet with corporate bureaucracy to get things done. Another advantage is that the owner of a business can handle service and not worry about turning it over to someone who will turn off a good customer or client.

Service literally covers everything in a small business operation right from the management attitude to and through the sale and the end result which includes the customers reaction.

Avoid negative service because if a customer has complained and has not been answered, or the management blames others for the mistakes, this will reflect negatively on the business.

Service means giving that added touch, that special gesture and that one step that puts you up front and one step ahead of your competitor. It's the little things that count. Most service is basically inexpensive. That service can include who answers the phone, who does the delivery work, the attitude of the sales people, and treatment by management.

Treat your customer or client as you would yourself. Here's a list of don'ts that can enhance any business:

- Don't leave a customer with the feeling that you are better than they are.
- Don't put the customer down, even if they reject your product or service.
- Don't overwhelm your customer with a sales pitch.
- Don't run down your competitor.
- Don't be so friendly that the customer can't stomach you.
- Don't rave about the features of your product or service to the point of being obnoxious. If it was so great it would be sold out. Your customer has common sense.
- Don't be deceptive in pricing your product.
- Don't brag about your accomplishments.

- Don't tell your customer how great you are.
- Don't try to impress your customer with how much money you make.

Take advantage of customer complaints

Turn a complaint into a positive action for your business. It's an opportunity to relate directly with that customer. If that customer receives good service on the complaint he or she is going to tell others how well they were treated. Once the complaint is settled it can be one of the best advertisements available. As a matter of fact, for a small business with a limited advertising budget, it can be the only effective method of advertising.

Cut costs of operation with word-of-mouth advertising

Bad-mouth advertising spreads like wild fire. It's quick and you have no chance to respond. The effects can ruin a business. I know of a restaurant that opened in March and by October it was closed because of bad-mouth advertising.

Sometimes we have a right to bad-mouth some businesses. For instance, I find some "big city" business establishments and large corporations that overlook service—airlines for one. In the "big city" often times hotels and restaurant people will treat their customers with disdain—it's called "upmanship." That's a universal complaint.

Some government agencies have a tendency to treat customers with rudeness and contempt. Being non-competitive you think they don't have to care—their job is secure and there's no way they can be replaced.

There are some businesses that are so successful they more or less tell you what they want and not what we want.

Those are the kinds of things that are bad-mouth advertising. This is the kind of advertising you don't need.

15

Creditors and Bill Collectors

THERE ARE ABOUT 3,400 COLLECTION AGENCIES AND BILL COLLECTORS. THEY are independently owned businesses and are located in every community throughout the country.

Collection agencies and what they want

Each and every one of these agencies is in business for one reason and one reason alone—to make money.

In an attempt to influence the public to think otherwise, the American Collectors Association tells us that if someone out there doesn't collect these past due bills, some $13,000,000,000 annually, the financial system in our country could become so disrupted that it could put a halt to the entire credit system. According to this association spokesman, "This could cause an adverse effect on everyone and we would all end up paying higher prices for services and products."

The public image of the collection industry

Because of the type of work they do the collection business has never been thought of in glowing terms by the public. In fact, one can almost look at the collection industry as being a scavenger of the credit-financial world. They are the ones cleaning up the mess left by those who don't take time to pay their bills.

The bad guy image of the bill collector

In order to collect these past due accounts, at one time bill collectors used every tactic they could. This often included harsh diplomacy, harassment, and even physical threats. There are still some collectors out there who believe they can hound a debtor to the point of breaking. They become so upset that they will pay the bill so they don't have to deal with that collector anymore. So, there is some justification for the perception the public has about bill collectors.

Despite the fact that there have been some changes taking place, the industry itself seems rather complacent about "fixing" or doing anything positively about that public image. The American Collectors Association recently tried to encourage their 3,400 members to pitch in and try and do something that could change their image. It was suggested by the association that each member throw in a few dollars and hire a public relations firm. The thought was that by hiring a PR firm their image could be improved through advertising. Sounded like a good idea, but do you know what the general membership said when asked for donations to the fund? In general they said, "Public relations doesn't affect the bottom line."

The changing image

Most of the aggravating and badgering tactics used by some collection agencies have been eliminated. Bill collectors aren't the old types we think of them as being—or at least they're not supposed to be. Changes have taken place.

Part of this image change has taken place because most collection agencies realize that the old tricks of brow beating until the bill is paid just doesn't work—and besides, a lot of these methods of collection are no longer legal. Not only are they illegal but most debtors know they can stop any threatening action simply by reporting any mistreatment to the state office of Consumer Affairs or file a complaint with the Federal Trade Commission.

One can argue whether this change has taken place because the collection industry wanted to change or that they were forced into this change because of the new laws that were passed regulating their collecting practices—namely the Fair Debt Collection Practices Act.

At any rate, today collectors and people working in the collection business are average ordinary citizens and responsible members of their respective communities. Some are active in the Rotary and Lions Clubs, Chambers of Commerce—and yes, they even go to church. They are in fact, human, and when treated decently, can be downright accommodating and helpful to those in need of help.

Working out the accommodations with the bill collector

A bill collector is trained to aggressively get payment in full with no excuses accepted. The motto of almost every collection agency is "payment in full." This means when you hear from a collector about a bill you owe they want the money and they want it right now. It's the job of that collector to:

- Convince you that you must pay your bill
- Overcome your objections to paying
- Counsel you to overcome financial barriers to paying your debts

Most of us sincerely want to pay our bills, but for a variety of reasons just don't seem to get around to it, or sometimes we just don't have the money and can't pay. But once that bill gets to a collection agency it certainly isn't going to be any easier and can become a most unpleasant experience to say the least. It's unpleasant because bills and bill collectors can raise our anxiety level. But it's also unpleasant because those unpaid bills can and will have a major impact on our credit buying.

So, if we've been confronted by a creditor or a bill collector, how can we cut a deal? Here are four suggestions that you might consider.

1. Don't get angry. Our first reaction when we get a collection letter or collection call is to get mad as hell. That doesn't help. There's no reason to get angry—at the bill collector, at the creditor, or at anyone else. In the most part it's a time to realize that there's only one person at fault. Getting angry doesn't do anyone any good. It's also time to adjust our thinking and realize that someone has done us a favor by giving us whatever it was and instead of being asked to pay cash we were given the privilege of using credit and taking a period of time to pay the obligation. When the collection letter or call appears it means that obligation was not lived up to. Now is a time when it's necessary to find a solution. Anger and hostility are not solutions.

   Remember, the collector usually has the upper hand. They too can become angry. If they become angry and you're angry you can imagine what this leads to . . . chaos, more problems and more anxiety.

2. Don't rely on excuses. If you think you can use excuses, they don't work. Most collectors have heard them all. Here's a list of those that have been tried and failed:

   - The check is in the mail.
   - I've already paid the bill.
   - I didn't order this and I'm not going to pay for something I didn't order.
   - I didn't get the bill.
   - I never received the merchandise.
   - I want to return the merchandise.
   - Don't bother me.
   - This is such a small bill it's not worth all this trouble.
   - If you don't stop harassing me I'll call my lawyer.
   - I'll send the check today.
   - I want to see the invoice.

   Excuses do not solve the problem.

3. Communicate, Communicate, Communicate. Usually when a bill has been turned over for collection it's a sign that all communication between the debtor and creditor has ceased.

    Once the bill is placed in the hands of a collection agency then communication must take place. A debt collector will usually communicate about the bill, will listen to the complete story, and through this communication will recommend and work out a solution. This solution will be something you can live with.

    But before the bill gets in the hands of a collector, communicate with the doctor, dentist, department store, bank, or whoever it is. That communication can possibly save you a lot of time, energy, and for certain, a lot of anxieties.

4. Ask for help. If the bill is a just and due obligation it must be paid. If this be the case then ask the creditor or the bill collector for help in getting it settled and paid. Evading the payment isn't going to help or do anyone any good. Whatever the reason is that the bill hasn't been paid up to this point, the matter must ultimately be taken care of. Find a solution by asking for help.

    If you firmly believe you don't owe the bill, tell that story in full to whomever you can get to listen. Provide complete details about the circumstances and be prepared to provide good solid evidence to support your claims. Simply by saying it didn't work isn't enough.

What to do about disputed bills

"I went to the garage, had my car fixed, I took it out on the road and on the first trip the transmission fell out. Now I'm getting dun letters to pay the bill."

"I took my dog to the veterinarian to be treated. Two days later the dog died. Now they want me to pay this bill and my dog is dead."

"My dentist fit me for a set of false teeth. They never did fit, now they're in my dresser drawer, and I'm getting billed for these teeth. I don't think I should have to pay."

"I joined a record club, took records for a year and then decided to quit. Since then I've been getting records and now bills for the records I didn't order. The last was a letter from some collection agency and they stated that if I didn't pay they would ruin my credit."

"I got my car fixed at the service station. I put the bill on my credit card. The car hasn't worked right since. Now I'm getting a bill from the credit card company and they're charging interest. I'm not going to pay the bill because I never did get the car to work."

"Last summer I had the cooperative fertilizer company spray my grain field for weeds. The sprayer went too far and got into the apple orchard and killed part of my apple crop. Now I got a letter from the collection agency that says they're going to take me to court if I don't pay the bill."

"My daughter went to the hospital emergency room for treatment. Now we're getting a bill for the hospital services and this was supposed to have been paid by medical assistance.''

''We rented an apartment and signed a lease. Because we had to move we left before the lease was up. Since we've heard that the apartment owner has rented the apartment. Now we're getting dunned by a collection agency for that rent. That means that the apartment owner is trying to collect rent twice. Is this right?''

''I went to the doctor for health care. When I got the bill I was astounded at the amount I was charged. Now they've turned the bill over to a collection agency. I don't think I should pay because the charges were too high.''

''My wife went to the doctor to get a shot. Since then she's had a numbness in her arm. The collection agency says we have to pay the bill regardless.''

There are of course endless stories about disputed bills. In every single case of a disputed bill there are always two sides to the story. One is the debtor who has received, by their perception, improper services or products. On the other hand is the creditor who has spent their time and money to provide the service or product.

In every single case of a disputed bill the reason the bill ends up with a collection agency is because communication between the two parties has ceased. Neither party wants to talk about it. Hence, the only solution to any disputed bill, regardless of the circumstances, is for communication to take place. This communication can be between the individual who owes the bill, the individual who has the money coming, the collection agency or a combination of any and all of the three.

If there's some give and take on the part of all concerned there's usually a solution. That solution can be in the form of a settlement or a payment plan of some sort.

If all else fails and if the dispute isn't solved through this kind of communication then the next best step, and this goes for any of the three parties, is to proceed through legal action. At that point the court will settle the dispute.

Avoid legal action: no one wins

Getting involved in a legal matter is not only time consuming, but downright expensive. The end result is that you have to pay the bill but there are often considerable hidden legal costs. Here's an example of a bill that went through legal action to collect:

Bank Loan Turned Over For Collection	$1956.58
Interest from Date Of Collection	419.95
Conciliation Court Filing Fee	18.00
Court Docketing Fee	10.00
Sheriff Execution Fee	5.00
Sheriff Service And Mileage Fee	32.00

The total collection paid by the debtor was $2441.12.

That's not the only cost. There's a considerable amount of personal involvement that can be embarrassing. For instance, the sheriff will drive up to your workplace and serve your employer with the execution papers. This means the employer will be advised that a portion of your forthcoming paycheck will have part deducted to pay on this obligation. A special check will be written to the sheriff to cover these charges. This of course takes time and a undue amount of inconvenience on the part of any employer.

If the bill isn't paid in full on this first execution then another garnishment will be served on the following pay check, and each consecutive pay check until the bill is paid. Each time there are the additional legal fees added which are paid off the top with nothing applied to the bill until the legal fees are paid.

The point is that any sort of legal involvement costs money and it's better to make a settlement through communication before it becomes a legal matter.

Conciliation court and the bill collector

The principal idea of conciliation court or small claims court is so each person can have their day in court without hiring an attorney. In theory this works pretty well, but if you're on the losing end it can be costly.

Here's the way it works. If someone owes you money you can file the claim with the clerk of court in your respective county. At the time of filing be sure and have a copy of the invoice as proof of the obligation. The clerk of court sets up a hearing at which time both parties appear before the judge and present their side of the story. The judge then makes a determination on the testimony and evidence.

If the judge finds the person does owe the bill he will grant a judgment. Remember, neither the judge nor the court collects the money.

In order to collect the money the next step is getting an execution which then goes to the sheriff and the sheriff will execute on the property or wages you advise him to act on. If the payment is made then the judgment is satisfied. That judgment remains a part of the individual's credit file for seven years, whether it's been satisfied or not.

Figure 15-1 shows a list of the various status and provisions those states have regarding conciliation or small claims court published by *Collector*, a monthly publication of the American Collectors Association.

Solving collection problems

Here are some frequently asked questions regarding collections, collection agencies, and bill collectors.

Q. Two years ago I had some accounts for collection turned over to the Credit Bureau. I paid them in full and now the Credit Bureau is still reporting this information whenever I apply for credit. Why are these collections that I've paid still being reported and used against me?

A. Accounts for collection, paid and unpaid, are in fact credit ratings—records of how you pay your bills. This becomes a part of your permanent credit history. They will remain on your record for seven years.

Simply because the accounts were paid doesn't mean they are taken out of

Avoid Litigation

SMALL CLAIMS COURTS: MONETARY LIMITS, ATTORNEY REQUIREMENTS

STATE	COURT*	MAXIMUM CLAIM	PROVISION	LAST KNOWN REVISION	ATTORNEYS ALLOWED/ REQUIRED?	COMMENTS
Alabama	Small Claims Court	$ 1,000	Statute	1985	Yes/No	
Alaska	District Court	$ 5,000	Statute	1986	Yes/No	
Arizona	Justice Court	$ 499	Statute		Yes/Yes	
Arkansas	Municipal Court	$ 3,000	Constitution	1987	No/No	
California	Municipal Court, Justice Court	$ 1,500	Statute	1986	No/No	
Colorado	Small Claims Division of County Court	$ 2,000	Statute	1987	No/No	If filer is attorney, opposition allowed attorney
Connecticut	Small Claims Session of Superior Court	$ 1,500	Statute		Yes/No	
Delaware	J.P. Court	$ 2,500	Statute	1986	Yes/No	
District of Columbia	Small Claims Branch of Superior Court	$ 2,000	Federal Statute	1984	Yes/No	
Florida	County Court	$ 2,500	Rule		Yes/No	
Georgia	Magistrate's Court	$ 2,500	Constitution	1983	Yes/No	System of deferred payment can be arranged if hearing avoided
Hawaii	Small Claims Court	$ 2,500	Statute	1981	Yes/No	
Idaho	Small Claims Division, Magistrate's Court	$ 2,000	Statute	1980	No/No	
Illinois	Circuit Court	$ 2,500	Statute	1981	Yes/No	
Indiana	Small Claims Division of Superior Court, Circuit Court, County Court	$ 3,000	Statute	1981	Yes/No	Attorneys required for corporations with claims over $300
Iowa	Small Claims Division of District Court	$ 2,000	Statute	1973	Yes/No	
Kansas	District Court	$ 1,000	Statute	1986	Yes/No	Attorneys allowed after judgment
Kentucky	Small Claims Division of District Court	$ 1,000	Statute	1980 or 1981	Yes/No	

Source: ACA Public Affairs Department, September 1987 survey
*J.P. Court = Justice of the Peace Court

Fig. 15-1. There are small claims courts for the ordinary citizen all over the country. This is a list of those courts and services provided.

SMALL CLAIMS COURTS: MONETARY LIMITS, ATTORNEY REQUIREMENTS

STATE	COURT*	MAXIMUM CLAIM	PROVISION	LAST KNOWN REVISION	ATTORNEYS ALLOWED/ REQUIRED?	COMMENTS
Louisiana	Small Claims Division of City Court	$ 2,000	Statute	1985	Yes/No	
Maine	Small Claims Division of District Court	$ 1,400	Statute	1954	Yes/No	
Maryland	District Court	$ 1,000	Statute	1987	Yes/No	Attorneys allowed for corporations with claims over $1,000. Claim limit $2,500 as of 1/1/88
Massachusetts	District Court, Municipal Court in Boston, Housing Court	$ 1,500	Statute	1984	Yes/No	
Michigan	Small Claims Division of District Court	$ 1,500	Statute	1986	No/No	Attorneys may represent themselves or corporations in which they are officers
Minnesota	County Court	$ 2,000	Statute		Yes/No	
Mississippi	Justice Court	$ 1,000	Statute	1986	Yes/No	
Missouri	Associate Circuit Division of Circuit Court	$ 1,000	Statute	1982	Yes/No	
Montana	Justice Court	$ 1,500	Statute	1987	Yes/No	
Nebraska	Small Claims Division of County Court	$ 1,500	Statute	1985	No/No	
Nevada	Justice Court	$ 1,500	Statute	1985	Yes/No	
New Hampshire	District Court, Municipal Court	$ 1,500	Statute	1984	Yes/No	
New Jersey	Special Civil Part of Superior Court	$ 1,000	Statute	1981	Yes/No	
New Mexico	Metropolitan Court, Magistrate Court	$ 5,000 $ 2,000	Statute	1981	Yes/No	
New York	Small Claims Court, Parts of City Court, Civil Court, Town Court, Village Court	$ 1,500	Statute	1981	Yes/No	
North Carolina	Small Claims Court	$ 1,500	Statute	1985	Yes/No	
North Dakota	County Court	$ 2,000	Statute	1985	Yes/No	Attorneys may appear by consent of judge
Ohio	Small Claims Division of Municipal Court	$ 1,000	Statute	1982	Yes/No	
Oklahoma	Small Claims Court	$ 1,500	Statute	1976	Yes/No	
Oregon	Small Claims Departments of District Court, Justice Court	$ 1,500	Statute		No/No	
Pennsylvania	District Justice Court, Philadelphia Municipal Court	$ 2,000 $ 5,000	Statute and Rule	1985	Yes/No	
Rhode Island	District Court	$ 1,500	Statute	1987	Yes/No	
South Carolina	Magistrate's Court	$ 1,000	Statute	1979	Yes/No	
South Dakota	Magistrate's Court	$ 2,000	Statute	1980 or 1981	Yes/No	
Tennessee	General Sessions Court	$10,000	Statute		Yes/No	
Texas	Small Claims Division, J.P. Court	$ 2,500	Statute	1987	Yes/No	
Utah	Circuit Court, J.P. Court	$ 1,000	Statute	1986	Yes/No	
Vermont	Small Claims Court	$ 2,000	Statute	1984	Yes/No	
Virginia	District Court	$ 7,000	Statute	1981	Yes/No	
Washington	Small Claims Court	$ 1,000	Statute	1981	No/No	
West Virginia	Magistrate's Court	$ 3,000	Statute		Yes/No	
Wisconsin	Circuit Court	$ 1,000	Statute	1978	Yes/No	
Wyoming	County Court, J.P. Court	$ 750	Statute	1979	Yes/No	

Source: ACA Public Affairs Department, September 1987 survey
*J.P. Court = Justice of the Peace Court

Fig. 15-1. Continued.

the credit file. Each time the Credit Bureau is contacted for your report this history is reported as factual information which includes the date they were paid.

Q. I received an injury while I was working. I was taken to the hospital emergency room. I didn't pay the bill because I thought it was going to be paid by my employer. Now it's been turned over for collection. Can you tell me why?

A. You obviously haven't communicated with your employer or with the hospital. Unless you've made arrangements with the hospital, your bill is due when you receive the service. Hospitals do not have a charge or open account policy.

If your employer has insurance the claim should have been filed, however, this is not the responsibility of the hospital.

The account has been turned over for collection and now becomes a part of your credit history. Pay the bill. Then work out the dispute with your employer. The hospital is an innocent bystander.

Q. I was treated by a doctor and was not satisfied with the service. The following month I had to be taken to the emergency room. Can the doctor I owe money to refuse service in the emergency room?

A. A physician cannot refuse treatment in an emergency situation if he or she has been assigned to be on call at the time. However, if the physician is not assigned to emergency room duty at the time of your call he is under no obligation to appear and make his service available.

Q. If I pay a disputed bill with a partial payment and write on the check payment in full can this check be returned?

A. Yes. Simply by sending a check of partial payment does not constitute settling the dispute. However, if you do send the check with it marked payment in full, and it is cashed then it becomes payment in full.

Q. I joined a book club. I tried to get them to stop sending books that I didn't want. I don't seem to be able to get them to stop. Now I'm getting statements for payments. What can I do?

A. If you made every attempt to stop the books and you duly notified them that you are not accepting any more, and they persist with collection letters, then contact your nearest Office of Consumer Affairs and give them full details.

I would also write a letter to the book club notifying them that you are writing to the Office of Consumer Affairs, or send them a copy of the letter. I think this will stop them.

I doubt that this account will ever show up on your credit record, despite their threats of ruining your credit. Most collection agencies do not list these types of collections with a credit reporting agency.

Q. I rented an apartment and because I had to move I couldn't give the landlord 30-day notice. Now I've been charged for another month of rent that I didn't occupy the apartment. In addition they are threatening to turn this over for collection. Can they do this and if so will it affect my credit?

A. Yes, they can do this and yes, this will appear as a collection on your credit record.

You must give proper notice when vacating an apartment regardless of the circumstances. Most states have a 30-day notice period and this usually means from the 1st to the 30 or 31st, not from the 5th to the 5th.

Q. How threatening can a collector be in trying to get me to pay a bill?

A. A collector's job is to get paid and he will use every method possible, within the law, to get the job done.

For your own peace of mind, if the bill is owed, pay it. The longer it festers the more difficult it becomes. Be honest with yourself and to the people you owe the money. After all, they helped you out when you needed the help. Now repay the favor.

Q. What effect will a judgment have on my credit history?

A. That judgment will appear in your file for 7 years. There are a lot of banks and loaning institutions, as well as credit card companies, who will not issue credit to anyone who has a judgment on their record.

That judgment is recorded in the courthouse and becomes a part of public record. If you own property those records are checked and in order to sell the property the judgment will have to be satisfied.

Q. I've been told that if I tell the collector not to contact me about a bill that means he can't call me again. Is this true?

A. Basically that is true, although it's not the smartest thing to do. If you cease communicating, almost every collector will proceed with legal action to collect that bill. This means more expense and a lot of hassle.

Q. I have no job. I don't own any property. I have no visible assets. What can a collector do about collecting a bill against me?

A. Nothing.

Q. I got a bill from a collection agency. It makes me mad because I had every intention of paying the bill when I could but the store just wouldn't wait. Now they've turned it over for collection, what can I do?

A. Every credit manager and every collector has to deal with people who make promises to pay. Here's what happens. When we buy a product from a store, all is well and good. We're happy with what we've bought, charged it, and have every intention of paying. But once the newness of the product is gone it's not so easy to pay. We think we can put it off and promise to pay, but don't. Then suddenly there's a collection letter. Here again is a case of failing to communicate, ignoring the bill and finding no solution. Get the bill paid because stalling will not benefit you or the store—only the collection agency.

Q. I have an insurance policy for my hospitalization. I took the papers to the hospital for them to fill out and complete for their payment. For some reason or another the bill wasn't paid in full and now the hospital is billing me for the balance. Am I responsible for payment if I have insurance?

A. Yes. The insurance contract you have is between you and the insurance company and not the hospital and the insurance company. It sounds like you have a policy that has a deductible clause or the insurance company doesn't cover everything you expected.

The hospital has provided service to you when they were needed and it is not their responsibility to pursue collection through an insurance company or through you. It is your responsibility to get the bill paid and then if you think you have money coming contact the insurance company.

Q. I've been told that if I pay $5 a month on a bill then the bill collector can't bother me and try to collect more. Is this true?

A. No, it is not true. Unless you've made arrangements with the person whom you owe money to accept the $5 per month, then the bill is past due and must be paid in full, not at the rate of $5.00 per month.

Q. I'm divorced and have custody of my three children. My husband has moved away. My divorce papers state that he is responsible for all medical and hospital bills for the children. One of the children was taken to the hospital emergency room. I have no insurance. The bill was sent to my husband for payment but they never heard from him. Now it's been turned over for collection and they want me to pay. Can they do this?

A. Yes. The hospital has no agreement between you, your children, and the hospital, which means the mother can be held totally responsible for payment of the child's care. The hospital has a right to be paid for their services. They do not have the time nor the money to become involved with family disputes of this nature. It is your responsibility. Pay them and then it's up to you, and your attorney, to go after your husband to get the money.

Q. I contacted a plumber to come into my home and do some work. I asked for an estimate and then hired him. When the bill came for his services it was almost twice what the estimate was. I refused to pay and now the bill has been turned over for collection. What can I do?

A. It sounds like you and your plumber have a communication problem. The first thing I recommend is contacting the plumber and finding out the reason for the extra charges. Was it possible that you asked for more work done than the original contract and estimate? My advice is to make a settlement. If that doesn't work then the only alternative is filing in conciliation court.

Q. I want sincerely to pay my bills but the medical bills we've had have really gotten out of hand. Now we're getting bills that we can't handle. What can we do?

A. It sounds like you do have a "hard luck" story. I'd recommend a visit with the doctor or hospital manager and tell them the truth. There's a chance they can work out a payment plan.

There's another thing to keep in mind when talking settlement of the bill. If the doctor or hospital have to use a collection agency they will have to pay them 33 to 50 percent of the bill. This is a time when maybe you can cut a deal and ask for a discount rather than them paying the collector.

Q. If I wanted to use a collection agency how much would I have to pay?

A. Each agency sets its own fees. Most charge between 25 and 50 percent of the total amount of the bill.

16

Gimmicks, Tricks and Credit Schemes

IF YOU'VE BEEN TOLD THAT THERE ARE METHODS AVAILABLE WHEREBY YOU CAN clear up your credit record and start with a clean slate, and you believe this, then I have a feeling you might also believe in the tooth fairy.

Believe me, this is a myth, despite what you might read in the various advertisements promoting credit clinic services. They state they can clean up your credit no matter how bad it is and put you back on the road to financial recovery, back to credit buying, new credit cards, and new loan availability—instantly and no questions asked.

Beware credit clinics: hang onto your purse strings

The credit clinics have led people to believe they can actually stop the credit system. Their deceptive advertising states:

- Erase Bad Credit! 100% Guaranteed
- Remove Bankruptcy, Judgements And Liens From Your Credit File

Figure 16-1 is a sample of their advertising. They certainly make it sound good. But the truth is that credit clinics cannot clean up your credit record. Nor can they remove any information from the credit file.

Credit clinics are in business for one purpose and one purpose alone and that is to get your money. They don't help those who are most in need of help—those people who are in financial trouble, and credit clinics don't provide one ounce of

Individual Service . . . . ($150.00).
Individual Service Where Bankruptcy Was Involved . . . . ($200.00).
Couple Service . . . . ($200.00).
Couple Service Where Bankruptcy Was Involved . . . . ($250.00).
Absence of Credit   ~m·. . . . . ($500.00).
5% Fee Where Y   ⌐ind Major Financing For You.
Consultation . . .   . (No Charge, Initial visit).
Credit Related M   **EXHIBIT**   . . . . (Negotiable).

TRW-TUC CREDIT DATA
ADDRESS
CITY, USA   DATE

(all services require adva
'refunds are made in ac
Absence of Credit Pro
r details.

ısitivity of the program please call

DEAR SIRS:
I AM REQUESTING THE ACCOUNTS AND SUBSCRIBERS
THAT I HAVE IDENTIFIED BELOW BE INVESTIGATED AS
THESE ARE NOT MY ACCOUNTS AND I WISH TO HAVE THEM
REMOVED TO REFLECT MY EXCELLENT CREDIT RATING

SUBSCRIBER   SUBSCRIBER #
J. C. PENNEYS   5784839
CURWAS 30-4   12-76
BANK OF TEXAS   ACCOUNT #
PD CHG OFF 9-80   7584839   8969 99503 9
WOULD YOU PLEASE FORWARD ME AN UP-DATED CREDIT
REPORT AFTER THE COMPLETION OF YOUR INVESTIGA-   758439920-99
TIONS.

CORDIALLY,
JOE CONSUMER
330 685-60-7584

Cashing of this check constitutes partial payment
on account(s) and requires bearer to withdraw
account(s) from any collection agency bein
utilized and further to delete and to cease list
or having listed by any means (including col
ion agencies) any data concerning this a
to any credit reporting agencies.

Fig. 16-1. *Credit clinics are a recent con game. Here are samples of advertisements found in many tabloid papers.*

public service. They are for all practical purposes a leech on the credit-financial system. One would be hard pressed to find a reason, other than greed, for their existence.

False claims lead to false hope

Most of these credit clinic companies claim they can help anyone with bad credit eliminate those negative ratings and purge judgements and bankruptcies from the file. But first, before they do anything, they need money—your money. In order to process their so-called clean up plan they charge a fee which can be anywhere from $50 to $2,000, depending on what the traffic will bear. And let me tell you, there's little difference between the $50 service and the $1,000 service because they can't perform the service they promise at all. They have absolutely no guarantee they can remedy any credit problem and there is no proof they can provide the services they advertise.

Here's how the scheme works. Once they get your money the credit repair company will advise you to contact your credit reporting agency and dispute all the ratings in the file, or they will have you sign a power of attorney form and they will contact the reporting agency and dispute the information.

The next step places the burden on the credit reporting agency. What this means is that according to Section 611 of the Fair Credit Reporting Act all disputed and challenged information is to be put on hold until it's verified. It cannot be reported.

When the credit clinics first started this it certainly put a burden on the credit reporting industry. A lot of the agencies were jumping through hoops for a while as people came running into their offices disputing information in their files. In fact, at first the reporting industry stopped in their tracks and didn't know what to do. This meant the credit clinics had their way and they surged ahead faster than lightning knowing they had caught onto a new gimmick which was primarily an easy source of money. Subsequently the credit clinics and repair companies grew by leaps and bounds overnight. There were no restrictions, no control, and no one watching over them. It was for all practical purposes open season on the credit reporting industry and credit grantors.

Part of this quick growth can be attributed to the fact that the credit reporting industry didn't act. They were caught sleeping, mainly because they weren't interested in any controversy or public exposure. The credit reporting industry more or less went right along with the credit clinics. It certainly wasn't planned that way, but that's the way it happened. No one put a stop to the credit clinic scam and they were able to operate freely.

Catching on and catching up stopped credit clinics

It wasn't long before the credit industry got its act together and saw what was going on. They took immediate steps to get this under control. The first thing they did, rather than putting these disputed ratings on hold, was check and verify the ratings immediately. Once the ratings were verified, the information and file was reactivated. This put a stop to those who thought they could get more credit cards because their file was put on hold. This meant that the waiting period, which was what the credit clinics depended on, was no longer existent.

Blackmail has backfired on the credit clinics

Once these clinics saw what was going on their next step was to advise the debtor, their client, to contact those business and professional offices who had turned their accounts over for collection and were never paid to offer 10 cents on the dollar as a settlement of the account, if the office would delete the rating and collection from their credit file. This trick, like the others, didn't work. The credit reporting agency does not and will not eliminate the ratings.

Do it yourself: it's easier and less expensive

Everything that a credit clinic can do you can do better, at no cost. You do not need a credit clinic to advise you to contact a credit reporting agency and dispute ratings. You can do this yourself. But remember, if those ratings are correct and verifiable you're not going to get them eliminated by a credit clinic, by yourself, or by anyone else for that matter. The ratings cannot be removed from the file.

Who gets hurt?

The sad part of this entire scenario is that the credit clinics direct their appeal to those who can least afford to spend money foolishly and those who need help the most. People in financial distress usually look for any help they can get and often times try to find an easy way out. The quick-fix credit clinics appeal to them because they think it's an answer to their problems.

But as anyone knows, it's extremely difficult to get out of credit trouble. Credit clinics will only add to the problem because it's a case of sticking good money after bad which leads to a financial bottomless sink-hole.

Here's the story of an individual who got caught in the credit clinic trap.

Jim, age 31, got himself into a lot of financial trouble through overspending. He bought an expensive car, a new boat and motor, a motorcycle, and other luxury items he didn't need. He got himself mortgaged to the hilt and had more payments than income. In addition his credit cards were filled to the limit. There were bill collectors hounding him and legal action threatened at his workplace.

In desperation he answered a credit clinic ad, ordered their services, and sent a money order for $350 (they won't take checks). He received a packet of materials from California. He should have known right away that anything from California was not going to help a simple country boy from the midwest. Anyway, he received information in this packet advising him of the steps to take to clear up his credit record. Of course the first was to notify the credit reporting agency where he lived that he disputed all the ratings—whether there was a dispute or not. Unbeknownst to him at that time, the credit reporting agency verified the so-called disputed accounts immediately. He was duly notified that the ratings had been verified and they could not be removed from the file.

Jim ended up with the same ratings, the same financial problems, bill collectors still trying to get him to pay his bills, and $350 less money. I asked him, "What did you learn from this experience?" He said, "I learned that I got taken for $350."

Check before
becoming involved with credit clinics

If you're still not convinced that credit clinics can't help you, the second bit of advice I have is to check this list before proceeding:

- Can that company be trusted?
- Does the firm have my best interests at heart?
- Does this firm understand my problems?
- Is the firm in business to help me solve my financial problems?
- After they get my money will they perform a service that I will be satisfied with?

- Does the company care about my financial concerns?
- If I have trouble after I've paid my fee will this company follow through and help me?
- Will they be friendly after they get my money?
- Do they realize that my financial problems are serious and that I need help?
- Am I searching in the dark and grasping for some quick answers?
- Am I taking this step out of desperation thinking there are no other solutions?
- Should I seek help elsewhere first?

After you've answered these questions to your satisfaction then talk to someone, a friend, a banker, an attorney, or anyone you can trust to give good advice.

Advice that can save you money

If you're in need of help, don't just sit and stew about your problems. If you really have disputed bills on your credit record go right now and get them cleared up. You don't have to pay a credit clinic or anyone to have this done.

If you've already paid your fee to a credit clinic and the results are less than what you had anticipated, which is most likely the case, contact the Office of Consumer Affairs in your state and file a complaint with the:

Federal Trade Commission
Washington, DC 20580

Report to them the complete details of your experience.

Laws are putting a stop to the credit clinics

About now you're probably saying, "If all these firms are so sleazy and are operating on the fringe of legality, how come they're still in business?"

Of course the answer to this question is that in a free society we can try anything, legal or illegal, until we get caught.

Credit clinics have certainly gotten the attention of a lot of people. Of course, they are a fairly new phenomenon and like anything else new it takes a while before they shake out and the truth surfaces. At the present time there's a considerable amount of attention being paid by state and federal legislators regarding the legality of the credit clinics. Some new laws being proposed are:

- An act forcing credit clinic companies to advise the consumer, the public, of their legal rights under the Fair Credit Reporting Act before signing a contract for the credit clinic services.
- A disclosure of all services the credit clinic can provide, including all costs.
- A time period which gives the consumer the right to cancel the contract.
- Require the credit clinics to post a surety bond.

- Prohibit credit repair companies from making misleading statements about their services, such as being able to eliminate the negative information from a file.
- Prohibit the repair company from counseling individuals and making misleading statements to the creditor and the credit reporting agency.

The state of Maine recently passed legislation that requires credit repair companies to post a $10,000 bond and to place any fees it collects in escrow until after the services have been completed.

Even the *National Enquirer* has issued warnings regarding credit clinics. In a recent article the headline read as follows:

"Beware! New Scam Offers To Improve Your Credit Rating"

This leaves us with a duck story. If it looks like a duck and acts like a duck it must be a duck. And if the National Enquirer says it's a scam, it must be a scam.

Credit doctors are an outright fraud

Along with the credit clinics there are credit doctors. Credit doctors claim they can improve the credit record of anyone. Here's how they work. The credit doctor establishes an all new identity which includes a new social security number, new driver's license number, and new credit cards. They search through garbage cans, post office junk boxes, bank statements, doctor bills, credit card billing receipts, and discarded charge slips. With this information they can build a "whole new person." This new-person identity then is sold to the individual who has a bad credit history and they can enter into the credit market with this new identity.

Beware of these schemes. They've been and are being investigated by the Secret Service.

So far as it is known the credit doctors have caused some $15,000,000 in bad debts to be charged off through this fraudulent method. In one case an individual using new identity was able to bilk $100,000 worth of fraudulent loans, including a home loan through the Veterans Administration.

In Houston a Federal Judge awarded $375,000 to an individual whose reputation was damaged by a credit doctor and the "doctor" was convicted and sentenced to 10 years in prison and fined $10,000.

A credit card scheme

A recent promotion, for those with various credit problems, is Citizens Gold I.D. Service Card. This company, according to their advertisement, will provide a card (not a credit card) for $10. According to this their Citizens Gold Card can be used to borrow up to $20,000 on just your signature.

Well, it's not quite that easy. As a matter of fact, the words and statements per se, in their promotional material, is not dishonest but is quite deceiving. What they are saying is that their card "can be used" to borrow up to $20,000, but it certainly doesn't guarantee credit or the fact that you will qualify for a $20,000 loan.

The key to their promotion is this:

"As a Citizens Gold Cardholder, you can take out your card from your wallet or purse anytime . . . for proof of identification to get the things you want."

That's it. The card can be used as an identification card—and no more. This card will not, and I repeat, will not, get you the things you want.

The point is that it's simply a gimmick. You've already got identification—drivers license, social security card, etc.

Further on in their promotional letter they state:

"Use your Citizen Gold I.D. Service Card for identification when you . . . take the keys to a new automobile . . . go to rent a luxury apartment."

They say nowhere in their promotion that this is a valid "credit" card, simply that it's an identification card. It cannot, and I repeat, cannot be used for credit purposes to buy a new automobile or rent a luxury apartment.

The primary message is:

"There is a small $10 CAB Administration fee—for processing name, printing, numbering, registration and validation."

The fact is this card has no credit benefits and would not be accepted by any store, bank, or anywhere for that matter as a charge card. Beware.

Loans by mail

The next scheme is loans by mail.

Here are some of ads taken from some of the tabloid newspapers:

BORROW $500—$40,000! "Overnight." On Signature. Keep indefinitely! Box 5499-B. Diamond Bar, California 91765.

BORROW $500—$100,000 No One Refused. Free Application. 750FS Johnson Hollow, Jefferson, North Carolina 28640

BORROW $500—$40,000! By mail. 97% Eligible! Any Purpose! Free Application. National, Box 7627-F. Long Beach, California 90807.

IMMEDIATE Loan to individuals refused elsewhere. No collateral, co-signers, interviews. 98% accepted! Associates, Box 98-F2, Brooklyn, New York 11235

Sounds great. No credit, no collateral, no nothing. I answered the ad to:

GENERAL ACCEPTANCE FINANCIAL SERVICES
Box 56359
Charlotte, NC 28256

First came a letter that said something like this:

Dear Friend:
Thank you for your reply. We can help you to get that loan you need.
Our loan program is one of the best in the country. No credit, Bad credit,
Bankruptcy does not matter. We can help . . . borrowing by mail can be
so easy and has so many advantages over conventional lending.
Fill out the enclosed loan service application. We can help.

With this letter there is a routine loan application with the following statement:

IMPORTANT: Fee must be included with application in order to complete processing. Enclose $25.00.

I sent the $25. In turn I received six pages with the names and addresses of
banks and savings and loan institutions all over the country. There were no further instructions. I assume the next step would be to contact one of these banks
and make application for a loan—and of course there's no guarantee that the bank
will give you a loan. But one has to admit that this company, for $25, did as they
promised and that is, "help you to get the loan you need."
    I contacted some of the banks and loaning institutions on their list. None had
heard of General Acceptance Financial Services and none were aware that they
were using their name on this mailing list.
    Want to save $25? If you're looking for a loan check the yellow pages in any
telephone directory.

17

Bankruptcy:
The Cure-All
. . . and Other Myths

HEAVY DEBTS AND PAST DUE BILLS CAN BE A VERY FRIGHTENING EXPERIENCE FOR anyone. Filing bankruptcy to eliminate paying these debts can be not only a frightening experience but emotionally devastating. Anyone thinking that filing bankruptcy is a piece of cake and a common ordinary everyday occurrence is making a grave mistake and is in for a rude awakening. The ill effects of filing bankruptcy are long and harsh. That bankruptcy can become a traumatic experience, but it also affects credit records, buying power, and future investment plans.

Canceling debts is not a joyous occasion

Filing bankruptcy should be considered an extreme measure that should be undertaken only if there are no choices. Those extreme measures could be the result of:

- Loss of a job and income
- An expensive illness
- A staggering financial setback
- A decline in property values
- A business investment turned sour

For those who have no choice and have become devoured in debt, the bankruptcy law permits those, if the petition is approved by the bankruptcy judge, to be relieved of the financial burden of the debts. This is the law.

But once that bankruptcy is approved it is filed in the county courthouse and becomes a permanent part of public records—public records that are open and available to anyone at anytime. In addition, that bankruptcy becomes a 10-year part of that individual's credit record. This then becomes a powerful force for any future credit dealings.

The warning signs that lead to bankruptcy

Anyone seriously in debt has already experienced the first signs of a potential bankruptcy and that is emotional strain. Once the worrying starts there is no let-up. That worry and anxiety can become overbearing and is something we carry with us day and night. That emotional strain is the first sign of trouble.

There are other signals which indicate a potential bankruptcy. Let's take a look at them along with potential solutions:

Problem: The inability to determine total indebtedness. Not knowing the total amount of bills and obligations, playing a guessing game, a monthly financial game of Russian roulette with the bills is a sure sign of financial trouble.

Solution: The first step is to sit down and go over your financial records. Know exactly who you owe, how much you owe, and the total payments due each month. Then accept the fact that something must be done—now!

Problem: Paying only a small payment on large bills. What this amounts to is paying $10 on a $75 payment or the minimum payment on credit card debts. This non-payment means trouble because there is an 18 to 20 percent interest charge on the unpaid balances. This only increases the debt load and obviously adds to the overall problem and not the solution.

Solution: The cause of the problem must be recognized and solved first, and that is: Stop Spending! Tear up the credit cards. Then, if at all possible, get those credit card balances paid in full as soon as it is financially feasible. Ask other creditors for more time to pay their bills. When you do, make certain you indicate that you have every intention of paying them in full.

Problem: Paying bills with money that should be used to pay other obligations. This is known as juggling the paycheck. Spending more than we make, and using savings to pay bills, is a symptom that must be resolved.

Solution: Analyze where the money is going each month and then find corrective measures to get spending under control. Buy only what is absolutely necessary and then cut that by 10 percent.

Problem:
Taking on two jobs to keep up the payments. Occasionally an extra paycheck comes in handy to anyone. However, if it gets to a point that there is a total dependency on a second job to keep afloat then it is no longer fun and it's time to take a look at the causes.

Solution:
When there is financial stress it is not a time to take on job burn-out stress. This only increases the overall pressure of everything else and adds to the anxiety burden—something no one needs when trying to solve financial problems.

If it is absolutely necessary to keep two jobs, do it only until all the obligations and bills are paid. Then devote work, time, and effort to the principal job and develop a program for position and financial advancement on that job.

Problem:
Being slow in paying bills each month. If everyday bills and obligations are not paid this means there is financial trouble ahead.

Solution:
Set up a budget and live within that budget. To cover any past due bills, contact those creditors and ask for their consideration and make a sincere commitment to pay back everything you owe. Most people will listen and cooperate when they know there is sincerity.

Problem:
Going on a borrowing binge. Going from one loan company to another trying to keep ahead of past due payments simply adds to the burden and solves nothing.

Solution:
Stop spending and stop borrowing. Seek a consolidation loan with one loaning institution and make a firm commitment that you will stop spending and will pay this obligation. Do not borrow to make payments on other loans. Don't buy any more useless things.

Problem:
Seeking loans from relatives and friends. This is a sign that the loan companies will no longer advance credit. Borrowing from friends and relatives can be the beginning of a last desperate stand.

Solution:
If friends and relatives will sincerely help that is fine. But if you ask for their help tell them the whole truth. Then make a firm commitment that you will repay them in full—no matter what, and even if you have to file bankruptcy. Don't wipe out friends and relatives in a bankruptcy.

Problem:
Being delinquent on taxes. Not having money to pay real estate or any other tax is an extremely serious matter. If taxes are not paid the government will come after you and if they do it can be embarrassing and costly. Remember, taxes can't be charged off on a bankruptcy.

Solution:
Not paying taxes is extremely painful because it is not only the burden of taxes, but there is a stiff penalty and interest added. Keep taxes paid.

Problem: Being denied credit. Sometimes this is a symptom of the last stand and is the end of credit and credit buying.

Solution: Turn this problem into a solution and look at it as a positive implication, at least for the time being. It means no more borrowing, which means no more spending, which means no more debt— which means peace of mind.

Problem: False pride takes over. It is very difficult for any of us to admit that we might have made a mistake or that we have troubles we can't handle. Rather than facing the problem we find it easier to ignore it, refuse to accept the fact that there is a problem, or to simply hate it.

Solution: Financial distress is a problem that must be faced no matter how hard we try to ignore it or how much we want it to go away.
            Don't let false pride get in the way of the possibility of finding a solution. Discuss the problem openly and freely and don't leave anything unsaid. Most people will understand and be helpful. It is much better to be humble and debt-free than it is to be proud and bankrupt.

Symptoms of potential business bankruptcies

All the symptoms of a potential individual bankruptcy apply to almost any small business. But there are some added warning signs and indicators that should be looked at.

Problem: Using gross receipts to pay operating costs. When a small business starts taking gross receipts to pay for the overhead expenses, such as heat, lights, rent or mortgage payments, and other fixed expenses, there is nothing left over to replenish the business itself.

Solution: This is a time when there is a dire need for a stringent budget that must be adhered to and followed closely. There can be no alternative. In that budget must be made room for capital to continue the business.
            This is a time when management can look at excessive spending. This may include eliminating country club dues, social clubs, luxuries, and all dues and donations. It means cutting down on a standard of living that is excessive and costly to a business.

Problem: NOT MEETING THE PAYROLL. If employees are not paid, employees will not stay on the job.

Solution: If necessary, cut unnecessary help. Do the mundane work yourself. Work nights. Ask your family to pitch in.

Problem:	NOT PAYING PAYROLL TAXES. The Internal Revenue Service reports that the major cause of small business failures and bankruptcies is not paying payroll taxes. Payroll taxes is not your money to spend. Payroll taxes is money that belongs to the employees and the government. It is not yours. Do not spend it!
Solution:	Cut the costs of the payroll wherever possible. Not paying payroll taxes is not a solution and is a crime. The IRS will quickly close the doors of any business that does not pay these taxes. Once the doors are closed there is no solution.
Problem:	Not paying suppliers. Not keeping current inventory bills paid means the potential end of a business. Suppliers demand their money and can quickly stop the flow of their products if they are not paid. If this does happen to any business it becomes a financial sink-hole.
Solution:	Cut spending, cut costs of operation that do not affect suppliers.
Problem:	Not paying utilities. It takes heat, lights, and all utilities to keep any business operating. Utility companies can shut off their services if the bills are not paid.
Solution:	Get spending under control.
Problem:	Overspending on remodeling. Real estate investors can often times get caught in over-spending and have so much invested in the property that there isn't room for sufficient return from the rents.
Solution:	When a $100 fixture will work just as well as a $500 fixture, buy the $100 one. Don't over-spend on construction and remodeling costs. Shop around.

This list could go on but each and every one of these symptoms can lead to bankruptcy if not corrected. Probably the most extreme decision anyone can make, regarding their financial lives, is deciding to file for bankruptcy. It not only affects buying power and our overall credit lives which can include homes, cars, and investment property, but it also makes a powerful emotional impact on our lives unless we are so callous that we just don't care.

But most of us aren't callous. Most of us are concerned people who got caught in our status symbols trap of over-buying and over-spending and then found out there is no way out.

Alternatives to bankruptcy

Despite the fact that we may have gotten caught in this financial squeeze there are some alternatives to bankruptcy. It may not be easy, it may not be what we would like to do, and it may demand our changing the lifestyle we've been accustomed to, but bankruptcy can be avoided, and should be if there is a choice. Let's take a look:

- Communication: We have talked about communication before in this book, however, the fact remains that a lack of communication is one of the prime causes of financial problems.

  A first step to solving financial problems is to set up communication. Ask for help. Tell the entire story and don't hold back any facts no matter how bad they might be. Get everything out in the open.

  Include in this communication the fact that any plan includes paying off all obligations.

  Set up a payment plan where these bills will be paid off, one that creditors can live with, and one you can live with.

  If that creditor knows they have a choice of going along with your plan and eventually getting paid, or not getting anything, there's no doubt they will work with you. Most creditors would rather have a slow payment plan than no plan at all.

- Help From A Credit Counseling Service: Credit counseling services do not charge for their help. For further information on location of these services write or call:

  National Foundation for
  Consumer Credit, Inc.
  Suite 601
  8701 Georgia Avenue
  Silver Spring, MD 20910
  (301-589-5600)

  If a credit counseling service isn't available, find an attorney who will assist you—one that won't recommend bankruptcy. Bankers also can be of help.

- Read and understand what bankruptcy means: Know full well what you are getting into. Have a clear understanding of the ramifications of what happens after bankruptcy. Don't believe in the myth that it is the answer to all your problems and that once it's over that's all there is to it.

- Get control of your financial life: Throw away all credit cards and refuse any new applications. Get your lifestyle under control. If you have an income that represents $40,000 a year and you are spending $50,000 a year, realize it's time to stop spending.

Does bankruptcy wipe the slate clean?

If you can't get spending under control and bankruptcy remains the only alternative there are some important facts that should be known. Bankruptcy does not necessarily wipe the slate clean. There are some serious obligations that cannot be included, such as:

- U.S., State, County, District, and Municipal taxes. The tax collector can pursue collection until you are in the grave—and if you do end up in the grave they can go after your estate.
- All legal liabilities, debts, and obligations taken under false pretense cannot be filed. For instance, if you know ahead of time that you are filing bankruptcy and then go out and charge, these later debts are being taken under false pretense. The bankruptcy judge will rule they have to be paid.
- Debts and obligations attributed to malicious personal or property injuries. If you know that you are at the end of the rope and the finance company is going to take your car and you decide to take a hammer and beat the hell out of the car, you can be held liable for the repair and loss to that finance company.
- Student loans.
- Child support.

Here is something else to keep in mind. As the assets are sold off, the money is used to pay these following bills first:

- Administrative and attorney costs of the bankruptcy.
- Wages. If you are an employer and owe past due wages, these are paid first.
- Taxes.
- Rent.

Bankruptcy: seven, eleven, twelve, and thirteen

And if there is no other way out, what bankruptcy options are there?

Chapter seven bankruptcy   Chapter Seven bankruptcy means that the individual who owes money gives up all rights to property. This property is then liquidated, sold, and the money received from the sale of the property is used to pay off creditors.

Property exempt from a Chapter Seven bankruptcy includes equity in a home, personal property, a car, and tools of the trade. Example: If you are a carpenter your carpentry tools are protected and cannot be included in the property for sale.

Property that is not exempt includes investment property, land and real estate, vacation homes, personal property such as jewelry or art objects, and stocks and bonds. It's pretty safe to say that those who file Chapter Seven do not have these kinds of assets. However, if you lie you can become liable for perjury and that means extra trouble.

Chapter eleven   Chapter Eleven bankruptcy covers a business going into and through a restructuring process. The business can remain intact and operating. However, creditors are put on hold and cannot pursue collection until every opportunity is given for the business to recuperate.

Chapter twelve   Chapter Twelve is an act covering farm bankruptcy. This covers only family farms with debts less than $1,500,000 and 80 percent of those debts incurred from the farm operation. Chapter Twelve is similar to Chapter Thirteen whereby the farm can set up a repayment plan.

Chapter thirteen   Chapter Thirteen bankruptcy is a plan set up by a bankruptcy judge whereby the debtor has requested time to make an honest effort to repay most or all of debts and obligations.

Under this plan payments are made from all disposable income which includes that income after food, shelter, and other necessities are paid for.

Chapter Thirteen covers debtors who have less than $100,000 in unsecured debts, such as credit cards and other bills, and less than $250,000 in secured loans, which includes car loans and other mortgages. Anyone with greater debts must file either Chapter Seven or Chapter Eleven bankruptcy.

Under Chapter Thirteen anyone who has co-signed a loan is still held responsible for that debt, but during the time of restructuring the creditor cannot pursue collection from the co-signer.

One benefit of a Chapter Thirteen bankruptcy is the fact that in most cases banks and loaning institutions will look at this as a sign of responsibility on the part of the individual. This will be taken into consideration on future loans—however, it will take time to rebuild that much-needed trust. One banker told me that sometimes it can take as long as five years before they will even look at a loan application from a bankrupt.

Bankruptcy and your attorney

Do you know why attorneys file bankruptcy for their clients? To make money, and it can be a pretty hefty charge. Attorneys make good money and if anyone believes differently they will also believe that buying stock in the Brooklyn Bridge is a good investment.

Always find out what the attorney fee is in advance so that you know how much money you will need. The attorney will almost always ask for the money in advance.

Some attorneys do not mention the fact that when you file bankruptcy that this becomes a part of a credit file. Also they will not mention the fact that this does not eliminate the negative and slow ratings from the file.

Who pays for bankruptcy

Do you know that from the year 1979 to 1982—just a few short years—the number of bankruptcies doubled. Since 1980 bankruptcies have increased at a rate of 12 percent each year and it is predicted that figure will increase to 15 percent.

You might ask, "What's the reason for the surge of bankruptcies, especially since 1980?" The main reason is that in 1978 there was a major revision of the laws which were passed to help people who were truly in financial trouble. However, along came the abusers and found out how to beat the system. Then in 1984 there were some protective amendments added to the bankruptcy laws and this helped eliminate the abusers.

Regardless, there are the victims of bankruptcy. Do you know who they are? You and I. Bankruptcies are not free. A lot of money is lost through bankruptcies and somebody has to pay. We do, in the prices we pay for merchandise and in the taxes we pay. The fact is, there is very little good that comes out of bankruptcies.

The bankruptcy abusers

We've spoken about the thieves and scoundrels before. They also exist in the bankruptcy world. One of the main reasons for bankruptcy fraud is that the laws have consistently been changed in favor of the bankrupt. It has become easy to file, easy to slip through the system, and there seem to be no checks and balances. The courts themselves are in such disarray that there is really no one watching.

There are those who get as many credit cards as possible, charge on all of them, and then file bankruptcy. Once they file no one will check. If anyone does check usually the attorney will recommend making a deal paying off those who check and contest the bankruptcy, while the others lose. That bankrupt can hide the assets, understate income, and overstate living expenses. No one checks.

Credit card companies have been getting hit hard on fraudulent bankruptcies. For instance, VISA and MASTERCARD had a husband and wife file for bankruptcy. They listed $143,000 on 42 Visa and Mastercard cards and $57,000 on American Express, Diner Club and Carte Blanche cards. The fraudulent part was that the husband went under 3 different names during a six-year period of time.

In another case a couple filed bankruptcy with $22,000 on 8 VISA cards, $9,600 on 6 MASTERCARD cards. After an investigation of the bankruptcy it was discovered that this couple was earning $3,262 a month with expenses of $2,133 leaving a surplus of $1,129 per month which could easily pay off the debts.

In another case a couple owed the IRS $39,000, and all other bills totalled $234,000. In their bankruptcy they declared $202,000 in assets. The bankruptcy investigation revealed that part of these assets included a motor home, an antique vehicle, a Mercedes Benz and a Cadillac, plus a condo in Hawaii. Incidentally, the debts of $234,000 included $32,000 on VISA cards and $1,000 on MASTERCARD. This is certainly not a case of financial hardship but a case of abusive spending— and also what might be referred to as a ''con'' job.

Most experts, bankruptcy judges, trustees, and lawyers report that 40 to 50 percent of all bankruptcies are fraudulent or abusive. It is a part of our white collar crime wave.

Because the losses have become astronomical and because there is an ever increasing amount of fraudulent bankruptcies the FBI has taken a much more serious look at what has been occurring. The problem is that there are more crimes than there are people to handle these crimes.

How to survive a bankruptcy

It wasn't long ago that we had such things as debtors prisons. In the past it was not unusual to hear that a debtor was beaten up by a bill collector. However, none of these solved any of the financial problems. Punishment didn't help get money and overall produced nothing but more harm.

And there is no doubt that there are times when life's battles get too intense and people get knocked around. One of these times can be during bankruptcy.

The fact that bankruptcy does not present a pretty picture, and that almost everything to do with bankruptcy is negative, in the end there are some benefits. For those who absolutely have no choice and truly are down and out here is what a bankruptcy can do:

- Provide Relief. Creditors and bill collectors will no longer pursue collection efforts.
- Clean Up All Debts. With a few exceptions—taxes, alimony and child support—all old bills and obligations are wiped clean from the record.

    There are some who have a moral responsibility to themselves, and do pay back creditors after the bankruptcy.

- Start A New Credit Record. It takes time, but if there is a true effort to keep bills paid, after the bankruptcy, a new record can be established. However, the bankruptcy remains on record for 10 years.
- Seek New Loans. A banker told me that once a bankrupt establishes a new prompt paying record they will look at an application. However, this takes time.
- Save Face. Creditors will no longer be calling at the workplace which is usually an embarrassing experience.
- Develop A New Self-Worth. This can be the start of a new emotional outlook on life and the beginning of a new and better self-esteem.
- Establish Self Respect. With time, a new financial life can be established built on trust, honesty, and integrity.
- A Fresh New Start. This means learning a lesson from the experiences and understanding the importance of a good credit and financial record. This also includes accepting the responsibility of paying all obligations as agreed. It also means avoiding all the pitfalls of financial distress.

Let's set the record straight

- Bankruptcy is not a laughing matter.
- Bankruptcy may seem like a good idea now, but it can be costly in the future.
- Bankruptcy can ruin your chances for a home or college education loan.
- Bankruptcy is not a cure all or quick fix for financial problems.
- Bankruptcy will not produce a better credit rating.
- Bankruptcy will remain on your credit record for 10 years.
- Bankruptcy is not a painless way to avoid paying obligations.

America the beautiful . . . and bankruptcy

On a per capita basis the following states file the most bankruptcies and the least. The number one bankruptcy state in the nation, on a per capita basis is Nevada, followed by Tennessee, Georgia, California, and Indiana.

The states wherein the least bankruptcies are filed are, number one Vermont, followed by Massachusetts, Connecticut, New York, and Pennsylvania.

This is a list of how many bankruptcies are filed . . . state by state.

18

Our Freedom to Choose

IT'S TIME NOW FOR SOME FINISHING TOUCHES. AS A STARTER, OF THE FINISH, LET me say that as we review all that has been said in this book, and if we take everything into consideration regarding our credit-financial system—the inequities and injustices, the abuses and abusers, the greed and avarice, the thievery, and the unscrupulous and conniving operators—our free-enterprise credit system works pretty well for most of us.

Our system works

There's no doubt that the credit system, like everything else in our free enterprise business world, has its strengths and its weaknesses. But in the final analysis the strengths and benefits far outnumber the weaknesses. And the greatest of all these benefits is to pick and choose those parts of the system that work in our favor. Let me tell you what I mean.

Our open-door, open-credit policy of our economy and financial system gives us the freedom to:

- Choose or reject any or all part of the credit system, simply by participating or not participating.
- Accept the privilege of participation in the credit system and use other people's money to buy products and services whenever and wherever we wish.
- Obtain one of life's greatest benefits, that of a college education, by using our credit system.

In addition to those freedoms, we have the inalienable right and the freedom to:

- Vehemently dispute and disagree with the inefficiencies and blunders of our financial system, as well as our overloaded bureaucratic governmental system.
- Complain about the inequities and injustices built into these systems.
- Change, with our vote, those inequities and injustices that do not please us.

Our freedom to move about as we please

But most important, and the most cherished of all our freedoms, is the freedom to move about in our society just as we please—within the limits of the laws of our country.

As we move about, we have the freedom to use our credit and buy any kind of car we want and can afford, or to buy the biggest and best house imaginable—if we can afford it. We have the freedom to increase our standard of living to any level we so desire as long as we remain within the system limitations—that limitation being the ability to pay for that standard of living.

And finally, and most profoundly, we have the freedom to use our credit and make as much money as we want. There is no one, and I repeat, no one holding us back, interfering or obstructing us from becoming as wealthy as we want.

The morality of making money

Regardless of what you might have been led to believe or what you have been taught in the past, there is nothing immoral about making money and accumulating wealth in our free-enterprise system—if it is done in an honest manner and not at the expense of our fellow human beings.

When I speak of the morality of making money, I mean that with the accumulation of that wealth there comes a responsibility to our fellow man. That responsibility is to live up to all of our social and economic commitments—if for no other reason than to gain our own peace of mind.

There are those who think that the wealthy and successful people in our society may not have a right to their rewards, and frankly, I would agree with this when that wealth has been made illegally. There are others who believe that profit represents evil, and this is true if that profit is made at the expense of others.

But in the most part, morality, money, wealth, and success can and do work hand in hand. Profit, wealth, and success have become and are a totally accepted part of the fulfillment of the Great American Dream. Money and success is a goal that anyone and everyone should aspire to and something we can all strive for. That's part of our freedom of choice.

Accept those freedoms with reverence

All of these freedoms should not be taken for granted and there is no doubt that they are worth preserving and protecting. I say this because the alternative is not a pretty picture. Those who do not experience the freedoms we speak of are not able to participate in the good things of life, enjoy the fruits of their labor, and acquire security and wealth.

I have good reason to say this because I spent some time in the Soviet Union where there are no freedoms. There is no middle class and there are no opportunities to accumulate wealth or to show even a modicum of success.

Credit and the ability to succeed

As we all know, in our country, we can acquire whatever we want on the basis of credit. In the Soviet Union there is no credit. There is no chance to buy a car, a house, a business, or any kind of investment. It's impossible to go into the department store and ask to charge it. There is only one store G. U. M. (Government owned and controlled), and there is no such thing as "charge it."

In the Soviet Union everyone is poor. Their standard of living is minimal and at best barely equals that of the United States back in the 1930s. It was, for me, like entering a backward time machine and returning to the way I lived in the 1930s and 40s—poorly.

There are shortages of everything including the bare essentials of life—food and clothing. Private housing and personal homes are non-existent in most places. There are 9,000,000 people living in Moscow and there isn't one private home, only apartment houses. These apartment buildings are lined up along the streets one after another, after another, ad infinitum. Even though there are thousands and thousands of apartment buildings there still is not enough housing for all their people so most apartments are occupied by two or three families—unheard of ever in our country.

Modern conveniences that we take for granted—refrigerators, microwave ovens, television, and cars are non-existent for the average Russian. Only a few of the upper class politobureaucrats (and they call it a classless society) can afford cars, fine clothing, and private apartments.

There is no such thing as going to the bank for a loan to finance a car, a home, or even a TV. And that's to say nothing about buying investment property or improving one's lifestyle.

Glasnost and peristroika, which means openness and rebuilding, will take years and years of changes before it ever reaches the level and standard of living we take for granted in our country. And before peristroika can take place it will be necessary to establish an entirely new monetary and economic system. This change must include an incentive program so that people will want to work and be able to enjoy the fruits of their labor, but not a system as they have where they work and the government enjoys the fruits of their labor. Well, that's their problem.

Take time to smell the roses

There is nothing we can do to change this outdated system of government, and it makes no sense in getting involved or concerned. Our concern should be that of a better existence for ourselves.

That betterment has come because we have been able to use our freedoms and accumulate those riches that provide us with the good things in life—that's good. It is also good to acquire wealth to enhance our security. It's good to experience a successful investment. It's good to rise above the average. And it's good to enjoy the material things in life.

But all of these accomplishments are meaningless if we don't take the time to know and appreciate the good things in life that money can't buy.

In other words, take time to smell the roses.

Index

Other Bestsellers of Related Interest

UNDERSTANDING WALL STREET—3rd Edition
—Jeffrey B. Little and Lucien Rhodes
Praise for a previous edition . . .
"One of those rare publications that delivers exactly what it promises . . . consistently good." —*Barron's*
Completely updated to reflect current investment vehicles, trends, and developments in the nation's financial markets, this book is both an introductory guide and a dependable reference. The authors explain everything from how shares originate to the complex principles of technical analysis. 272 pages, Illustrated. Book No. 3686, $9.95 paperback only

SOLD BY OWNER! Secrets of Selling Your House without a Broker's Fee—Maurice Dubois
This practical guide gives you all the information you need to sell your home, coop, or condo *without* a real estate broker. Packed with information, *Sold by Owner!* provides step-by-step instructions outlining the entire process. You'll learn how to: size up the local housing market, use creative financing options, advertise, and complete necessary legal forms and contracts. 240 pages, 32 illustrations. Book No. 30016, $14.95 paperback only

LENDING OPPORTUNITIES IN REAL ESTATE: A High Profit Strategy for Every Investor
—James C. Allen
Earn high yields at low risk by making short-term secured loans! This book offers specific advice and procedures for investing in short-term loans secured by real estate. Samples of actual forms involved are included. Topics addressed cover: preparing a personal financial statement, sources of free advice, borrowing investment capital, setting rates and terms in any market, advantages of smaller notes, avoiding foreclosure, and "prospecting" made easy. 192 pages, 42 illustrations. Book No. 30019, $14.95 paperback, $24.95 hardcover

THE SMALL BUSINESS TAX ADVISOR: Understanding the New Tax Law
—Cliff Roberson, LLM, Ph.D
The most extensive changes ever in the history of American tax laws were made in 1986. And to help you better understand these changes, Cliff Roberson has compiled the information every small business operator, corporate officer, director, or stockholder needs to know into a manageable and readily understandable new sourcebook. 176 pages. Book No. 30024, $12.95 paperback only

GREAT AD!: Low-Cost, Do-It-Yourself Advertising for Your Small Business—Carol Wilkie Wallace
If you have big plans but a small budget, this book will help you to produce an effective, professional, and economical advertising campaign. It takes a hands-on approach and walks you step-by-step through research, media planning, and creative strategy. *Great Ad!* helps you research the competition, assess your business image, analyze the market, target your audience, schedule sales, and develop a media calendar. You also get hints on sources for artwork and music. 352 pages, 36 illustrations. Book No. 3467, $19.95 paperback, $32.95 hardcover

SITE SELECTION: Finding and Developing Your Best Location—Kay Whitehouse, CCIM
"I highly recommend it . . ."
—**Roger B. Baumgartner,** Realtor, CCIM
"This book is long overdue . . . much needed guidance and information . . . a must for anyone preparing to . . . invest in real estate"
—**A. J. West,** Director of Franchising Development, Denny's Incorporated
Whether you're a businessowner, investor or real estate professional responsible for locating potential business sites, this book will help you spot the pit-falls that can turn a seemingly beautiful piece of property into a financial disaster. 192 pages. Book No. 30053, $21.95 hardcover only

GETTING OUT: A Step-by-Step Guide to Selling a Business or Professional Practice
—Lawrence W. Tuller
A management consultant and former business owner, the author brings 25 years of buyout and acquisition experience to bear on the problems of establishing a "getting-out" position. He offers a complete and authoritative treatment of the subject for owners of any size business—as well as doctors, lawyers, accountants, and other professionals in private practice. 320 pages, 30 illustrations. Book No. 30063, $24.95 hardcover only

FRANK CAPPIELLO'S NEW GUIDE TO FINDING THE NEXT SUPERSTOCK
—Frank Cappiello

"Frank Cappiello is one of America's most brilliant securities analysis . . . he has few peers as a super stock picker." —Louis Rukeyser

Investors today still marvel at the huge profits made in superstocks of the past such as Xerox, IBM, and Hewlett Packard. For savvy investors, such opportunities still exist. In this new guide, Frank Cappiello reveals his own successful approach to uncovering the superstocks of the future. He shows readers how to sift through the thousands of available stocks and pick out the few that are poised for hypergrowth. 208 pages, 102 illustrations. Book No. 30041, $12.95 paperback only

INSTANT LEGAL FORMS: Ready-to-Use Documents for Almost Any Occasion—Ralph E. Troisi

By following the clear instructions provided in this book, you can write your own will, lend or borrow money or personal property, buy or sell a car, rent out a house or apartment, check your credit, hire contractors, and grant power of attorney—all without the expense or complication of a lawyer. Author-attorney Ralph E. Troisi supplies ready-to-use forms and step-by-step guidance in filling them out and modifying them to meet your specific needs. 224 pages, Illustrated. Book No. 30028, $16.95 paperback only

CREDIT AND COLLECTIONS FOR YOUR SMALL BUSINESS—Cecil J. Bond

Here's a practical guide for busy entrepreneurs and credit managers that tells how to set up or overhaul a small credit department. Includes forms, applications, letters, and reports ready to be copied and put to use. 192 pages, 66 illustrations. Book No. 30035, $18.95 paperback, $28.95 hardcover

SUCCESSFUL BUSINESS PRESENTATIONS
—Joseph A. Quattrini

This sourcebook shows you how to become more effective at communicating orally at all levels—with your peers, superiors, suboridinates, and customers. Quattrini shows you how to plan, organize, and deliver information in every conceivable speaking situation: proposals, demonstrations, lectures, committees, oral briefings, interviews, negotiations, discussion groups, debates, telephone sales, and more. 200 pages. Book No. 30055, $15.95 paperback, $24.95 hardcover

WHY EMPLOYEES DON'T DO WHAT THEY'RE SUPPOSED TO DO AND WHAT TO DO ABOUT IT—Ferdinand F. Fournies

". . . honest, concise, and immediately applicable methods" —Chris Marlin, Training Director, Buick-Oldsmobile-Cadillac Group

Getting employees to do what they are supposed to do is probably the biggest challenge for any manager. Ferdinand F. Fournies, internationally known business consultant and author, here shares innovative, yet practical ideas on how managers can prevent the most common reasons for employee nonperformance by preventive management. 120 pages. Book No. 30064, $8.95 paperback, $14.95 hardcover

COACHING FOR IMPROVED WORK PERFORMANCE—Ferdinand F. Fournies

". . . a solely needed guide/help book for salesmarketing managers." —*The Sales Executive*

Over 70,000 copies sold in hardcover; now available for the first time in paperback! By one of the nation's best-known business training consultants, this book shows you face-to-face coaching procedures that allow you to obtain immediate, positive results with your subordinates. Filled with examples, case studies, and practical problem-solving techniques. 224 pages. Book No. 30054, $12.95 paperback only

AVOIDING PROBATE: Tamper-Proof Estate Planning—Cliff Roberson

Discover how to hand down everything you own to anyone you choose without interference from courts, creditors, relatives, or the IRS. In this easy-to-read planning guide, attorney Cliff Roberson shows how you can avoid the horrors of probate court. Sample wills and trust agreements and checklists in every chapter make planning each step easy. *Avoiding Probate* covers: living trusts, life insurance, specific property, wills, family businesses, valuing your estate, estate taxes, and more. 263 pages. Book No. 30074, $14.95 paperback, $29.95 hardcover

THE ENTREPRENEUR'S GUIDE TO STARTING A SUCCESSFUL BUSINESS—James W. Halloran

Here's a realistic approach to what it takes to start a small business. You'll learn step-by-step every phase of business start-up from initial idea to realizing a profit. Included is advice on: designing a store layout, pricing formulas and strategies, advertising and promotion, small business organization charts, an analysis of future small business opportunities. 256 pages. 97 illustrations. Book No. 30049, $15.95 paperback only